"If you are curious about how biblical optimism could reform the missional posture of the church, then *Leaving Left Behind* is your go-to resource. This book provides a biblically rooted, culturally relevant, and application-based pathway to better understanding how positivity can advance the mission of the church. Instead of embracing a 'get me out of this world now' posture, Wilson makes the case for believers to embrace a 'keep me in the world now' mentality. You will be inspired to embrace God's mission and give God your best—right here, right now."

—Ed Love
Director of Church Multiplication for The Wesleyan Church

"Amidst an epidemic of pessimism, anger, and fear, Mike Wilson offers *hope*, not just for the local church but for the world Jesus died to save. His positivity, however, is rooted in something deeper than human progress or prosperity theology—it's anchored in the Scriptures and the saving work of Christ."

—Joshua M. McNall
Professor of Theology, Oklahoma Wesleyan University

"When an old car is restored, its value becomes obvious and its purpose restarted. There is some code in our nature that I believe God purposefully put . . . a code that values taking something broken and getting it working again. Mike's book will help you see an incredibly viable approach to restoring what is broken in the church, but even better, how restoring it can actually get restarted what God intended to be happening all along."

—David Kinnan
Lead Pastor of Fountain Springs Church

"We live in a culture that has been beat up enough, and the church does not need to add to this. Mike Wilson provides a framework for an optimistic outlook that the Bible provides. The message of the church should be about hope, grace, and a positivity that produces a passion for progress. Mike's emphasis on 'grace-focused teaching' is energizing. As he shares, 'The goal of the church is not to separate from culture, but to shape it.' Culture is best shaped through the optimistic message of redemption. Mike provides this message."

—Phil Stevenson
District Superintendent of the Pacific Southwest District of The Wesleyan Church

"Mike Wilson reminds us that the pessimism of the American evangelical church has led us to a grossly myopic view of our culture and our salvation, driving far too many to turn away from Christianity at just the moment when they need it most. *Leaving Left Behind* is a powerful wake-up call for pastors and churches alike, pressing us out of the mire of cynicism and directly to the hope and joy of Jesus Christ."

—Jennie A. Harrop
Author of *The Jesus Quotient*

Leaving Left Behind

Leaving Left Behind

How Positivity Will Help Christians Flourish

MIKE WILSON

Foreword by Leonard Sweet

WIPF & STOCK · Eugene, Oregon

LEAVING LEFT BEHIND:
How Positivity Will Help Christians Flourish

Wipf & Stock
An Imprint of Wipf and Stock Publishers
199 W. 8th Ave., Suite 3
Eugene, OR 97401

www.wipfandstock.com

PAPERBACK ISBN: 978-1-7252-8220-9
HARDCOVER ISBN: 978-1-7252-8221-6
EBOOK ISBN: 978-1-7252-8222-3

01/15/21

Contents

Acknowledgments

To MY WIFE, DARCI, you are the most faithful, strong, and beautiful woman I have ever known. Your selflessness will never cease to amaze me. No one really knows me unless they know you. To my sons, Lincoln and Titus, I don't do anything without thinking about how it will help you become the men God created you to be. You will do great things for God. Serve him.

Dad, God speaks to me through you. Billy Wilson, I follow you. Isaac Smith, thank you for showing me what leadership should look like. Paul Baughman, thank you for your support and wisdom. Leonard Sweet, you changed my mind.

God, make me a reflection of you.

Foreword

Say "Yes!"

ONE IN EVERY NINE people on the planet goes to bed hungry each night.[1] What is more, one in three of the world's population suffers from some sort of malnutrition on a daily basis. But those figures only relate to physical food. There are other kinds of food as well, such as food for the mind, food for the spirit. The soul can be as malnourished as the body. If one considers the food of being appreciated, affirmed, thanked, or the malnourishment of recognition, then the majority of the world's population goes to bed starving and debilitated every night. Especially Christians.

How many followers of Jesus diligently and selflessly serve the church, help the needy in some way every day, and lay down exhausted on their pillows at night without any cushion of thank yous or applause of recognition ringing in their ears? The worlds of business, entertainment, education, medicine, and the arts are better at acknowledging and celebrating their members than the church. What is our problem?

Mike Wilson has highlighted a root cause of our preferential option for the negative, our eagerness to denigrate more than celebrate. Many Christians read their Bible as "In the Beginning was the Word, and the Word was 'no.'" The do's and don'ts of the Christian life have majored in the don'ts and minored in the do's. How many of us grew up with the mantra "Don't drink, don't smoke, don't dance, don't chew, and don't go with girls who do?" This don't over do focus has created a flip-flop faith within a culture of the negative.

To be sure, some of the don'ts are valiant attempts at negative identity formation, showing us how to be in the world but not of the world

1. See the Food Aid Foundation statistics, as found in https://www.foodaidfoundation.org/world-hunger-statistics.html.

by showing us what the opposite looks like. I once heard a sermon on "A Church With Piles" where the preacher taught the congregation what it meant to be a Christian: Christians don't "pile on" the sick and wounded, don't kick when a person is down; Christian's don't "pile up" treasures on earth; Christians don't "pile in" the bandwagon and follow the fads of fashion.

Even if you were spared a childhood of don'ts, you went to school where if a teacher asked, "What do you think?" you were being asked to be a critic, to be a voice of against. To be critical about critical thinking, to be against is itself to be critical. But we are instructed to study to "show ourselves approved," and that divine approval does not come from "quarreling about words," which "only ruins those who listen," but from "rightly dividing the word of truth," which has a positive not negative impact on people (2 Tim 2:14–17).

"Eat freely!" came before "Don't eat of that one tree!" And there were a thousand "Yes, eat of that tree" to the one "No, not that one." It is not without significance that God made two generations (40 years) wean their grumpiness and complaining spirit out of the Hebrew gene pool. It took two generations to restore a state of confidence and courage and to get the Hebrew people to say no to negativity (Deut 1:6–7). We underestimate the unimaginable significance of an incarnational imagination where to enter a deeper experience with God you don't remove yourself from the world but you enter the world, in all its complicity and complexity, and find in the midst and mess of things a jubilee of joy, the very heart of God.

Jesus is defined as "God's 'yes!'" (2 Cor 1:20). "In the beginning was the Word, and the Word was yes!" Every person is God's yes to life and love. The church's default mode is critique and fault-finding ("I find no fault with this man," said Pilate). The Jesus default mode is one of hospitality and affirmation. As I teach my students, celebration precedes cerebration. You have no right to critique any author or any person until you can first celebrate that person's position or personhood as a gift, unique and special. Always celebrate before you cerebrate. You can make a good living by judging and critiquing; you make a great life by imagining the new, uplifting the neighbor, and celebrating the stranger.

There seem to be three Christian bents: pooh-pooh Christians, oom-pah-pah Christians, and umph Christians. Pooh-pooh Christians are negative, disdainful, holy hecklers of life. They look on each other with what

Flannery O'Connor called the "ice-pick eyes" of accusation[2]. Oom-pah-pah Christians are lock-step, legalistic soldiers in the Lord's army whose faith is flat and monotonous. Mike Wilson has written a book to show us how to be umph Christians, a people filled with vitality, verve, conviviality, and positivity.

Jesus is God's yes! Wilson's *Leaving Left Behind* shows us how to be yes people in the best and only true sense of that word. In this doom-and-gloom world of pandemic pandemonium, this book is a boom-bloom-and-zoom godsend of hope and promise. It is a book timed "for such a time as this" (Esth 4:14).

—Leonard Sweet

Best-selling author (most recently Rings of Fire), professor (Drew University, Portland Theological Seminary, Tabor College, Evangelical Seminary), and founder and chief contributor to preachthestory.com

2. O'Connor, "Parker's Back," 154.

Introduction

The World Needs the Church

GENERALLY, ANGRY AND FEARFUL churches die, but hopeful and coura-geous churches flourish. The Christian church in the United States is ex-periencing a temporary period of stagnation, largely due to an epidemic of negativity and infighting. That negativity has led to dogmatism, judgmen-talism, hypocrisy, and pessimism, and has added to the image problem that continually repels pre-Christians. The common self-critiquing statement that Christianity has become known more for what it is against than what it is for identifies part of the error that has led to the image problem that burdens the Christian church, but it stops short of diagnosing the full spec-trum of the limiting effects of negativity.

In vision-casting, tone matters. Reversing the judgmental and pessi-mistic tone of the Christian church will lead to a decline in the number of people who fear rejection from the church. As fear of rejection and judg-ment decline, the positivity that results will produce energy and growth as it has in the past. While it is true that pessimism and cynicism have put Christians at a disadvantage in the competition for souls, it is also true that the church is not dying. Worldwide, the church is actually growing rapidly, and it will continue to grow. Despite the damaging effects of the widespread adoption of "left behind" theology (an endtimes theology usually referred to as dispensationalism), Christians have reason to be optimistic about the potential of an American Christian revival.

Dispensationalism has convinced many Christians that the world will be destroyed before long-term discipleship strategies can work, and the pessimism that has resulted is repelling pre-Christians. No one trusts a sinking ship. Realistic optimism, on the other hand, is an effective tool in accomplishing goals, and it is a common attribute of the most successful

Christian evangelists. It is energizing to remember that the fearmonger-ing *Left Behind* books are not part of the biblical canon, and the church does have a bright future after all. This book will make the case that bibli-cal optimism for the future of the Christian church is both warranted and beneficial.

POSITIVITY

Although New Life is not a megachurch, it is the largest church in our county. Because of that, there is no shortage of people outside our congre-gation who tell me what I should actively take a stand against. Some people believe I should regularly warn our people that the end of the world is near, that my message should be one of fear of fire. Many people have told me to encourage people to prepare for some kind of apocalypse by stocking food, weapons, and gasoline. Even though Scripture speaks more about not worrying than it does about preparing for the worst-case scenario, I have been told I need to spend more time warning people about the antichrist and the mark of the beast. I have been told I should take a stronger stance against alcohol and gay marriage. I have been accused of talking too much about love and Jesus and not enough about the wrath of God. We are called to lead people to Christ, but fearful messaging has caused many people to doubt that we even follow him. We can't ignore sin, pain, or persecution, but those warnings must be led by hope and grace.

Jesus broke through cultural barriers by eating with sinners while the rest of the religious community judged and condemned them. The apostle Paul broke through cultural barriers by finding common ground with worshipers of false gods, and he learned that skill from Ananias, who welcomed a killer to the faith. Peter and Cornelius were able to get past their differences to become Christian brothers, and the greatest evangelists in Christian history have perfected the art of biblical hospitality. I grew up around churches that preached so much disdain for the world that they scared most of the kids I grew up with away from the church.

Happy People

It has been well documented that positivity leads to success.[1] This is a not a promise of prosperity without effort or inevitable success, but a person who utilizes the benefits of biblical optimism will achieve more than he or she could without them. Sonja Lyubomirsky, author of *The How of Happiness*, argues that happy people show "more flexibility and ingenuity in their thinking and are more productive in their jobs. They are better leaders and negotiators and earn more money. They are more resilient in the face of hardship, have stronger immune systems, and are physically healthier. Happy people even live longer."[2] Shawn Achor contends that happiness leads to success in almost every area of life, including marriage, health, friendships, community involvement, creativity, jobs, careers, and businesses.[3] Positivity will be a marker of the next great American revival, just as it has been in past revivals. Christian theologians who deny the hopeful message of Scripture are leading their Christian followers to unnecessary failure because they doubt the potential for success.

What convinces some people that success is possible in the first place? To discover why some people were able to persevere when faced with seemingly impossible odds but others failed to recognize solutions and gave up, Achor researched the mindset of people who worked in similar circumstances but came to different conclusions about perseverance. In *Before Happiness*, he writes,

> The reason some people were thriving while others—people in the exact same situation—were stuck in hopelessness, was that they were literally living in different realities. Some were living in a reality in which happiness and success seemed possible, despite the obstacles. Others were living in a reality where it was not. After all, how could someone expect to achieve happiness or success when stuck in the mindset that neither was possible?[4]

He concludes success is only possible if people change their reality—the entire lens through which they viewed their world—and believe success is possible. If Christians want to be successful, the worldview of Christians

1. Lyubomirsky et al., "Benefits of Frequent Positive Affect," 803.
2. Lyubomirsky, *How of Happiness*, 24.
3. Achor, *Happiness Advantage*, 41.
4. Achor, *Before Happiness*, xv.

should be a positive worldview, because positive Christians will be more successful in their mission to make disciples.

Positivity, Not Prosperity

Prosperity preachers must not be the only purveyors of positivity. My invitation to positive thinking is not an invitation to a prosperity gospel that treats positivity as a mysterious recipe for guaranteed success.

Matthew tells us Jesus told his disciples, "If any of you wants to be my follower, you must give up your own way, take up your cross, and follow me. If you try to hang on to your life, you will lose it. But if you give up your life for my sake, you will save it. And what do you benefit if you gain the whole world but lose your own soul?" (Matt 16:24–25). As Christians, our goal is not wealth or health; our goal is to become who God created us to be, and he created us to be the hands and feet of Jesus. For some, that goal will be more difficult and painful than for others, but when we face trials, God will give us peace to endure. In Philippians 4:7, Paul writes, "And the peace of God, which transcends all understanding, will guard your hearts and your minds in Christ Jesus."

Positivity is not a magical spell that conjures mystical forces to produce supernatural results. It is a state of mind that leads to success when it leads to diligence. UFC fighters train for months or even years before they fight. In other words, they fight their opponents hundreds of times in their head before they step into the ring. Belief that they *can* win encourages them to push forward, work harder, and even take risks. The same is true for employees working for a raise, students studying for a test, and pastors preparing a sermon. When we believe we *can* succeed, we work hard to achieve that possible outcome, but that is very different than believing we *will* succeed. If we believe we *will* succeed, we may be tempted to take it easy, to lose faith when setbacks cause doubt, and to avoid risks.

Fear

Anxiety levels in Americans are rising.[5] People are worried about the future, and, although almost all of the evidence shows otherwise, they feel like things are getting worse. Evan Osnos of *The New Yorker* reports

---

5. American Psychiatric Association, "Americans Say," line 1.

preoccupation with the apocalypse is flourishing, from groups of religious doomsayers to Silicon Valley.[6] Some people expect future disaster to come about as a result of technology. Some blame the media, the stock market, the government, or another pandemic. Others point their fingers at nuclear weapon stockpiles or global warming.

In an important statement about pessimistic Christians, Trevin Wax, author of *This is Our Time*, writes,

> Every generation believes that things are getting worse when compared to the past. Every generation adopts, at some level, a variation of the myth of decline or the myth of progress . . . In the church, we are tempted to scour the annals of church history looking for the pinnacle of better times, from which we have fallen and now must reclaim. Perhaps it's the early church, the Golden Age of the ecumenical creeds, the Reformation and Puritan era, or the revivals of North America. Whatever point in time we pick, we contrast ourselves to our ancestors and feel as if we've fallen from those heights. The world, and too often the church, is getting worse, we say. But all of this is a myth.[7]

Humans tend to judge the progress of the world based on the worst of current circumstances, and although that emotion is produced by uninformed thought, it is occasionally helpful when it leads people to search for solutions to problems. However, when it leads to pessimistic retreat and bunkering, it is counterproductive. Obviously tensions rise during pandemics, times of war and political insecurity, and rapid technological change, but humans have relentlessly adapted. Previous generations feared things we no longer fear, but we have adopted new fears in their place. "Doomsday—as a prophecy, a literary genre, and a business opportunity— is never static; it evolves with our anxieties. The earliest Puritan settlers saw in the awe-inspiring bounty of the American wilderness the prospect of both apocalypse and paradise."[8] And how do people who believe the worst about the future react? They build bunkers, and they prepare to fight.

Is all of this fear warranted? No. The reality is almost every statistic measuring health, comfort, war, famine, knowledge, and freedom reveals that the world is a better place to live today than it has ever been before.[9]

---

6. Osnos, "Doomsday Prep for the Super-Rich," para. 3.

7. Wax, *This is Our Time*, 2752.

8. Osnos, "Doomsday Prep for the Super-Rich," para. 42

9. Cliff, "This is the Best."

Unfortunately, health and peace without Christian joy don't usually lead to happiness. Positivity is not a result of comfort or peace. So why do we cling to negativity when we fear the loss of comfort and peace?

Peace that transcends all understanding and Christian joy must not be dependent upon the absence of immorality or physical threats of danger. There are times on this earth that it will appear to be more like heaven, and there are times that it will appear to be more like hell, but Christians are commanded to stay joyful and patient through both seasons. These difficult periods are what Paul calls "terrible times" (2 Tim 3:1). The word "times" is translated from the Greek word *kairos*. The ancient Greeks had two words for time, *chronos* and *kairos*. *Chronos* is ongoing, measurable time, while *kairos* is qualitative—it measures moments and seasons.[10] In other words, they will be like periods or moments, a temporary existence.

If we want God to purify the world, we can't be surprised when the world is singed by fire. Psalm 66:10–12 says, "You have tested us, O God; you have purified us like silver. You captured us in your net and laid the burden of slavery on our backs. Then you put a leader over us. We went through fire and flood, but you brought us to a place of great abundance." If the silver is not refined, it will not reach its full potential. The refining of the world can be seen as decline, or it can be seen as a necessary step in the purification process. As the world is refined, the pain will produce progress.

It seems Jesus even instructed us to submit to our political and governmental leaders. Would it not be logical to assume God would do a refining work in their lives in order to make following them realistic? Paul said in Romans 13:1, "Let everyone be subject to the governing authorities, for there is no authority except that which God has established. The authorities that exist have been established by God." It requires a significant amount of faith and optimism to believe God is working through our governing authorities.

Christ's Hopeful Message

Philippians 4:8 says, "Finally, brothers and sisters, whatever is true, whatever is noble, whatever is right, whatever is pure, whatever is lovely, whatever is admirable—if anything is excellent or praiseworthy—think about such things." Paul's advice to the Philippians is eternally applicable. Unfortunately, the Christian church has attached itself to creeds and statements

10. Valentine, "Chronos & Kairos," para. 3.

of belief, such as the Apostles' Creed and the Nicene Creed, that neglect statements of love and of actions that reflect the fruit of the spirit.[11] Those creeds do not reflect the ministry and teachings of Jesus. Using a teaching style rooted in stories, Jesus entered the long narrative of history to inject a gracious gospel that placed others before self. The image problem of the church cannot be separated from this lack of Christlike messaging.

Jesus did talk about a "narrow door" to his kingdom, but to avoid exaggerated worry, he immediately followed it with a statement about people coming "from the east and west and north and south, and will take their place at the feast in the kingdom of God," and his pessimistic language about those who fail to enter was directed at his contemporaries (Luke 13:24–29). About the church's "image problem," Chris Hillman Brown pointed to the importance of reflecting the language of Jesus by focusing on the prophecy concerning the "radiant" future of the church and its calling to be "a city on a hill" not the "judgmental or disparaging tone" of the American church.[12] The church's image problem cannot be separated from the extreme difference in tone between Jesus' graceful language and the church's cynical language, and it would be unwise to ignore the ideas and values that most evidently display that image problem. Jennie Harrop writes, "Christians have a horrible reputation—and the sooner we acknowledge the depth of the pain, distrust, and anger, the better equipped we will be to humble ourselves to a new way of loving others well."[13]

Disconnection

When the number of those people who considered themselves to be Christians grew large enough in the United States that they could use political means and majority rule to advance the Christian mission, they gave in to that temptation.[14] In *Christians in the Age of Outrage*, Ed Stetzer writes that since the values and practices of Christians shaped culture for so long, "they had the impression that they owned the culture in some sense. These Christians want their country back, and by that, they mean they want their cultural power back."[15] This caused Christians to see people disconnected

11. Leith, *Creeds of the Churches*, 678.

12. Brown, "Why Christianity Has an Image Problem," para. 15.

13. Harrop, *Jesus Quotient*, 419.

14. Hansen, "We Must Not Play," para. 13.

15. Stetzer, *Christians in the Age of Outrage*, 10.

from the church as the opposition rather than "sick" people in need of the Savior (Mark 2:17). The desire to see those people in the way Jesus saw them led Leonard Sweet to optimistically refer to people who are disconnected from the Christian church as pre-Christians.[16] It is good to mourn sin and pain in the world. Christian tears are necessary and inevitable if they believe biblical warnings about such sin. "Blessed are those who mourn" (Matt 5:4). But that mourning must not turn into pessimism. About that sort of pessimism, Trevin Wax writes:

> An overly pessimistic view of the world leads to a defensive posture. A defensive posture leads to defensive decision-making. We start making decisions based on maintenance rather than mission. Holding on to what we have holds us back from moving forward in faith in the power of the gospel. The gospel blows up pessimism. If you truly believe the Word of God has authority—that it will accomplish God's purpose and will not return empty, if you truly believe that God has a church and that the gates of hell will not prevail against it, then you fortify yourself for spiritual *battle*, not for surviving a spiritual siege.[17]

Our mission, or commission, is to "Go into all the world and preach the gospel to all creation" (Mark 16:15). And we know "repentance for the forgiveness of sins will be preached in [Jesus'] name to all nations" (Luke 24:47). It appears the dominant Christian narrative in America today is that living in the last days means we are doomed to fail in that mission, although few would admit that is the conclusion to which the narrative leads. It is depressing to be doomed to failure, and a group doomed to failure has very little curb appeal.

The Local Church

After college, I moved to Olathe, Kansas, one of the fastest-growing cities in the country, to help my brother plant a church. For over three years, we poured blood, sweat, tears, and money into that church. We tried everything we could think of to reach people with the gospel message, determined to grow by introducing pre-Christians to Christ and not to grow by relocating people from other churches to ours. However, just a few years into the effort, having run out of resources, energy, and hope, we closed the

16. Sweet, *Soul Tsunami*, 50.

17. Wax, "Pessimistic about the Future?," para. 8 (italics original).

church. It was demoralizing, and as a result of that experience, I lost faith in the local church model. Soon after that, I quit going to church altogether.

After a few years of rebellion against my calling to serve the mission of the local church, a friend invited me to his church, and I eventually joined that thriving congregation that at the time was called LifeChurch.tv. Hearing testimonies of life-change at LifeChurch.tv renewed my excitement about the potential of the local church. Since then, I have had the opportunity to serve a healthy church in Gillette, Wyoming that has solidified my belief that the church is God's plan to help people respond to the coaxing of the Holy Spirit. No other institution has been able to or will be able to accomplish tangible change in communities around the world like a healthy local church.

When a person loses faith in the church's ability to accomplish the Great Commission, that person will usually give up the mission altogether. Initially, they may tout a desire to make disciples by other means, but apart from the local church, no method of evangelism and discipleship has worked on a large, sustainable scale. These failures lead to doubt, and if there is no hope of success, effort wanes, fingers are pointed, and defensive bunkers are built. Pessimistic Christians put themselves in bubbles and focus on self-preservation, and when the mind is clouded by feelings of frustration and regret, a person's interpretations of biblical prophecy begin to lean toward the pessimistic possibilities.

In 1995, Tim LaHaye and Jerry B. Jenkins, with good intentions, released a wildly popular series of books called *Left Behind*. The series was an allegory of what the authors believe will happen before, during, and after the second coming of Jesus Christ. The series of books taught readers that in the future, the world will decline into extreme immorality, the influence of the church will decrease, and the antichrist will lead the world away from God. Christians read *Left Behind* similar to the way they read C. S. Lewis's allegories and Jesus' parables. The problem is the creative theology taught in the *Left Behind* books leads readers to an attitude of peril about the future of the church, and doubt about the future success of the church will actually lead to that dreaded failure.

When COVID-19 struck the world with fear, many Christians turned to their pastors and asked, "Does this mean the rapture is going to happen soon?" Western Christians have been trained to believe that increasingly hard times will signal the end of time, but they fail to recognize that when compared to most of human history our lives are easy and long-lasting. The church is suffering from an epidemic of pessimism, believing the future will be worse than the past, but Scripture's picture of the future is neither apocalyptic doom and gloom nor a psychological prosperity gospel. It is a call to biblical optimism, believing in the viability of revival. Every generation adopts a variation of the myth of decline, but the fear that is produced by that myth diminishes success. Almost every measurement of health, peace, knowledge, and freedom shows the world today is a better place to live than it has ever been before, and while Christians cling to fearful predictions of the future, the growing field of positive psychology provides evidence for biblical optimism, optimism that is grounded in prophetic truth, situational awareness, and unwavering faith.

Most Christians doubt a widespread revival is possible, but if we stop believing revival is possible, we will stop sowing for it. The resulting complacency will give way to pessimism and cynicism that will become a self-fulfilling prophecy.

CHRIST COMMUNITY CHURCH

In 2010, at a time when Christ Community Church (CCC) had become one of the largest churches in a small suburb in Missouri, their pastor, Caleb, resigned. Jonah, the pastor who succeeded Caleb, had an attractive personality and an above-average communication ability, but by 2013, the average worship service attendance of CCC had drastically declined. When denominational leaders recognized the numerical decline, their investigation uncovered an unfortunate change in tone at CCC. When the church was successfully reaching many unchurched people with the good news of God's love, the tone of the ministry was one of hope and hospitality, but Jonah had become engrossed with the goal of behavior modification. His sermons focused on the substantial rise of sinfulness in the world and the need for the church to separate from society. When it was determined that Jonah's messages had become too legalistic, the denomination asked Jonah to resign. After a significant political battle, Jonah did leave the church, but he and half of the congregation of CCC started another church in that same small suburb. The new church was called Solid Rock Church (SRC). SRC prioritized the pursuit of holy living. Five years later, due to an internal dispute, the worship pastor of SRC and half of the congregation left SRC to start another new church in the same suburb. However, after hiring a new pastor, prioritizing community involvement, practicing extravagant hospitality, and setting optimistic evangelism goals, the congregation at CCC experienced growth and energy like never before.[18]

Although this may be an extreme case, it is an example of a problem that has stifled church growth in America. This book will reveal that the positivity and hospitality of CCC is more effective and biblical than the pessimism and judgmentalism of SRC.

AN OUTLINE

Chapter 1 of this book will introduce the church to positive psychology, and it will reveal that positivity leads to success, not the other way around. Chapter 2 will reveal the negative effects of pessimism and negativity. Chapter 3 will show that negativity has given Christianity an image problem, and it will show how the adoption of an optimistic message of hope and grace can reverse that problem. Chapter 4 will make the argument that negativity leads to division. Chapter 5 will discuss the impact that pessimistic theologies have had on the church, and chapter 6 will debate the validity of those theologies. Chapter 7 will give guidelines and justification for optimism within the church. Chapter 8 will demonstrate that in order to be known for what it is for rather than what it is against, the church should graciously reach out to millennials and Generation Z with language they can understand, while being less distracted by arguments about secondary theologies. Chapter 9 will show that if the church follows the lead of optimistic Christian leaders like Jonathan Edwards, it will foster a spirit of excitement for the future of the church, rather than feelings of anger and a need for seclusion. The book will then conclude with some next steps and final thoughts. The church must allow positivity to open its eyes to the full range of future evangelistic possibilities. While the church in the United States is numerically declining, there is much reason for optimism and that optimism itself will be part of the solution.

DISCUSSION QUESTIONS:

a. Are you generally an optimist or a pessimist?

---

18. This is a true story, but the names, dates, locations, and some details have been changed in order to preserve the privacy of those involved.

b. Does it resonate with you that positive people are more successful? Can you think of any specific examples of positive people who are successful?

c. How do you feel about progress and human history? Is the world improving or declining?

d. Why do you believe anxiety and pessimism are rising in America despite the fact that standard of living is improving?

1

Positivity Leads to Success

More than any other element, fun is the secret of Virgin's success.[1]

—RICHARD BRANSON

I HAVE FOUR SIBLINGS, and one of the things I remember most about growing up was the chaos that occurred when our family traveled. After hours of frustration, trying to get everyone packed and in the car on time, we were barely on speaking terms, but without fail, my father took the opportunity to frustrate us even more by asking in a loud, obnoxious voice, "Is everybody happy?" It was his catchphrase. I'm not sure if he said it to annoy us or to point out we were obviously not happy, but he was very good at revealing our lack of happiness. After a few years, I discovered I could lessen the frustration of those moments by choosing not to respond emotionally to Dad. Instead, I ignored him, pretended to pinch the heads of the people in other cars, and asked my mom if we were almost there. Dad didn't like it when the family wasn't happy. He knew anger and frustration could ruin the vacation, but his method of cheering us up was not very effective. The problem is my dad's catchphrase was actually more likely to make us mad than to make us happy. Telling people to be happy when they are upset does not usually improve their mood.

---

1. Humphrey, *Effective Leadership Theory, Cases, and Applications*, 200.

This book will attempt to make you a more positive person, not by telling you to be positive, but by giving evidence that optimism is warranted and beneficial. We aren't shooting for delusional, pie-in-the-sky, blind optimism. We believe God has given us plenty of reason to be positive and even optimistic. Our goal is also not to send the message that we have arrived. Even though we believe success is possible, we have not yet reached our goal. Believing success is possible encourages people to push toward the goal, but believing we have already arrived leads people to complacency.[2]

The benefits of positivity do not justify false prophesy of unrealistic achievement, but even when realistic hope is warranted, human nature drags us toward fear and pessimism. This book is an invitation to biblical optimism that is grounded in hope and faith in God. In Jeremiah 28, Hananiah son Azzur delivered an optimistic message of hope to the people of Israel, but his message was a false prophesy. Jeremiah's prophesy in chapter 29 was just as optimistic as Hananiah's, but it was a message from God. This book will draw optimism from the words of God, not from a desire for growth, and that biblical optimism will help the church achieve the prophesied outcome.

In *The Happiness Advantage*, Achor writes, "the more you believe in your own ability to succeed the more likely it is that you will."[3] If Christians are going to take advantage of the benefits of positivity, they will first need to believe there is plenty of reason to be optimistic about the future of the church.

That kind of optimism leads to confidence, and confidence is valuable in self-motivation and in leadership. Victor Lipman writes, "In hard or uncertain times, of which there are many, employees want to be guided by a leader who projects confidence. It sends the right calming message, as do its close first cousins, resilience and optimism."[4] Confidence is a leader's best friend, and it is intricately connected to positivity. Tony Schwartz writes, "Confidence equals security equals positive emotion equals better performance."[5] In Luke 18, when Jesus told the parable of the persistent widow who would not take no for an answer, he was encouraging his followers to have confidence in God and pray with persistence. It is faith in God that should lead Christians to pursue our commission with confidence.

2. Achor, *Before Happiness*, 21.

3. Achor, *Happiness Advantage*, 74.

4. Lipman, "Why Confidence is," para. 5.

5. Schwartz et al., *Be Excellent at Anything*, 133.

I became the lead pastor at New Life Gillette Church in 2017. I was 33 years old. I had zero experience as a lead pastor, but I thought I could do it. I thought, "Sure it's a big church, but I've led staffs and helped lead big churches in the past," but I was blindsided by the weight of actually being in charge. The fear of failure, and the weight of decisions overwhelmed me. A few months after becoming the Lead Pastor, I was teaching a membership class, and in the middle of teaching, I lost vision. I literally couldn't see. I was upright and awake, but I had a headache and couldn't see. I pretended that nothing was wrong. I took some deep breaths and kept talking. After a few seconds I could see again. I assumed it was a fluke and didn't think much about it until it happened again at the exact same time the next day, and the next day, and the next. For weeks, every day I had the same strange episode at about the same time. I would get a pounding headache followed by temporary blindness. I had never experienced anything like it before. Eventually my doctor told me I was having a nervous breakdown that was causing optical migraines. During that year, our church's statistical numbers declined for the first time in many years. The church needed me to be confident, to take risks, and to cast vision of a bright future, but that's hard to do when you are overwhelmed by doubt and fear. That's when I started thinking about quitting my job, but before I made that decision, I decided to take a few days off to go to Cheyenne, Wyoming to talk to some friends, Andy Hazelet and Jeff Maness. They encouraged me. They told me with God's help I can do it. They told me they have experienced similar fears, and that encouragement, mixed with some extra time in prayer, made the strange episodes go away. When I regained some confidence (also because New Life began to show signs of growth), I was a better teacher and a better leader. I was also a better father and husband.

POSITIVITY COMES FIRST

Lyubomirsky et al., use the terms "positive psychology" and "positive affect" to imply a general sense of happiness and optimism. They write that "the characteristics related to positive affect include confidence, optimism, and self-efficacy; likability and positive construals of others; sociability, activity, and energy; pro-social behavior; immunity and physical well-being; effective coping with challenge and stress; and originality and flexibility."[6] Achor

6. Lyubomirsky et al., "Benefits of Frequent Positive Affect," 804.

writes an appealing introduction to the beneficial effects of optimism and happiness. He says,

> For untold generations, we have been led to believe that happiness orbited around success. That if we work hard enough, we will be successful, and only if we are successful will we become happy . . . Now, thanks to breakthroughs in the burgeoning field of positive psychology, we are learning that the opposite is true. When we are happy—when our mindset and mood are positive—we are smarter, more motivated, and thus more successful.[7]

Happy people show "more flexibility and ingenuity in their thinking and are more productive in their jobs. They are better leaders and negotiators and earn more money. They are more resilient in the face of hardship, have stronger immune systems, and are physically healthier. Happy people even live longer."[8] Is it any wonder Nehemiah said joy produces strength (Neh 8:10)? Advocates of church success would have no problem recognizing the benefit that would result if Christ's disciples and clergy exhibited those characteristics, and as advocates of the gospel and representatives of Jesus Christ, all Christians would increase their effectiveness if they were consistently and lastingly happy.

The most successful people, those people who just seem to always get lucky, are almost always those people who are most positive. For them, happiness isn't something they hope to have someday—it is a necessary commodity of the journey. In general, they get farther in life, and they have more fun doing it. This is not to say all success is achieved entirely by positivity, but it is one of the most helpful and universal tools available for achievement and perseverance. "Study after study shows that happiness precedes important outcomes and indicators of thriving."[9]

So why has the world failed to recognize the benefits of positivity, or what Achor calls "the happiness advantage?" A majority of psychologists agree with the findings of Achor, but the business world, political and religious leaders, and educators cling to their false idea that success leads to happiness and not the other way around. Many workers say happiness is a necessary casualty of success, and for some, happiness is even seen as a weakness. As they avoid it, they continue to drown themselves in effort,

---

7. Achor, *Happiness Advantage*, 37.

8. Lyubomirsky, *How of Happiness*, 24.

9. Lyubomirsky et al., "Benefits of Frequent Positive Affect," 804.

perhaps hoping for happiness, while those who are most happy pass them on the ladder of success.

In "The Benefits of Frequent Positive Affect: Does Happiness Lead to Success?" Lyubomirsky et al. analyzed the results of over 200 studies performed on almost 275,000 individuals and discovered happiness leads to success in almost every area of life, including marriage, healthy friendships, community involvement, creativity, careers, and business efforts.[10] They conclude that "research on well-being consistently reveals that the characteristics and resources valued by society correlate with happiness."[11] But it is not correlated in the way most people assume. Most individuals assume "success makes people happy." The opposite is true.[12] Happiness and positive emotions, like optimism, "lead people to think, feel, and act in ways that promote both resource building and involvement with approach goals."[13] When optimism is the predominant emotion a person feels, the person is led to see things in the world that are going well, and when all is going well, people can "expand their resources and friendships; they can take the opportunity to build their repertoire of skills for future use; or they can rest and relax to rebuild their energy after expending high levels of effort."[14]

Worry

Most successful people have learned how to temper worry. Achor says "the belief that worrying will prevent bad things from happening is one of the greatest enemies of positive genius."[15] Christians should have no problem with that statement, as it so closely reflects a statement made by Jesus in his Sermon on the Mount: "Therefore do not worry about tomorrow, for tomorrow will worry about itself. Each day has enough trouble of its own" (Matt 6:34). Jesus' proclamation has been proven by many modern-day scientists. Researchers at Harvard and other institutions discovered anxiety destroys the proteins at the end of our chromosomes called telomeres. This

10. Lyubomirsky et al., "Benefits of Frequent Positive Affect," 803.

11. Lyubomirsky et al., "Benefits of Frequent Positive Affect," 803.

12. Achor, Happiness Advantage, 803.

13. Elliot and Thrash, "Approach-avoidance," 804.

14. Fredrickson, "Role of Positive Emotions," 218.

15. Achor, Before Happiness, 176.

change rapidly accelerates the aging process.[16] On the other hand, when people spend time focusing on positive feelings for a few minutes, they significantly lower their levels of worry and pessimism. This does not only decrease anxiety; it also raises performance on tests of memory and critical skills by 10 to 15 percent.[17] Worry is crippling. Confidence and optimism are freeing.

Celebration

Another effective aspect of positivity is the importance of celebration, joy, and appreciation. Too often, success is celebrated too little while failure is bemoaned too much. Taking time to appreciate accomplishments is not only gratifying, "it also leads to better performance."[18] Tal Ben-Shahar and Angus Ridgway point out "one of the best ways to enhance positive emotions and restore energy is to write about positive experiences."[19] A primary benefit of success is the gratitude that can be shown after a victory. Messages of appreciation contribute significantly to the happiness of the giver and the recipient. They also improve the relationship of the parties involved. This concept should introduce us to the benefits of celebrating successes in our prayers. Emmons and McCullough performed studies that demonstrated how writing down things for which we are grateful each night before going to bed leads to higher levels of happiness and optimism, as well as to better performance and improved health.[20] If the church continues to encourage a theology that doubts the potential of successes to be celebrated, a lack of celebration will stifle growth and create an inability to recognize potential successes.

PERCEPTION

Believing a goal is achievable helps people achieve that goal. In addition, perception of the difficulty of reaching a goal affects an individual's ability to hit that goal. "Changing how you perceive the size of your target—that

16. Ahola et al., "Work-Related Exhaustion," para. 4.

17. Ramirez and Beilock, "Writing about Testing," para. 26.

18. Ben-Shahar and Ridgway, *Joy of Leadership*, 79.

19. Ben-Shahar and Ridgway, *Joy of Leadership*, 79.

20. Emmons, *Thanks!*, 36.

is, how you perceive the likelihood of success—can have the same cognitive benefits as increasing your perceived proximity to it."[21] In an experiment published in 2012, golfers were asked to putt a ball into a hole. The researchers then used other, larger circles to create an optical illusion that made the hole look smaller, and the golfers' success rate declined. Then they used smaller circles to make the hole look bigger, and the golfers' success rate improved. Even though the hole size never changed, the golfer missed their mark more often when the target was perceived as more difficult to hit.[22] Perception affects performance.

Only when individuals choose to believe they live in a world where "challenges can be overcome, our behavior matters, and change is possible can we summon all our drive, energy and emotional and intellectual resources to make that change happen."[23] Individuals whose brains are more regularly focused on positive thoughts have a greater chance of succeeding, and individuals who believe success is possible are more likely to find the path to success. Those people are not blind to the negative realities of life, but they also recognize they have the potential to do something about it. Social scientists have long discussed the true predictors of success. They disagree about whether grades in school, standardized testing scores, physical attractiveness, work ethic, emotional intelligence, or mental intelligence is the best forecaster, but most agree all of these matter to a certain extent. And it is a person's mindset, his or her grit, that knits all of these qualities together. The question then becomes, "how can we learn to harness and apply all of the various intelligences?"[24] Success is not about how much intelligence you have. It's about how much of that intelligence you believe you can use to accomplish something desirable.[25]

The positivity Jesus and Paul advocated for is more than blind happiness or irrational optimism. It is optimism rooted in an individual's power to accomplish something. The famous analogy of the half-full or half-empty glass paints a picture of an optimist who sees the current situation as good and a pessimist who sees the current situation as bad. There is, however, a third option. A successful person will seek a pitcher of water to fill the glass. Achor labels these people "positive geniuses," people who

21. Achor, *Before Happiness*, 122.

22. Witt et al., "Get Me Out," 397–99.

23. Achor, *Before Happiness*, xvi.

24. Achor, *Before Happiness*, 7.

25. Achor, *Before Happiness*, 11.

can see a great range of opportunities, possibilities, and paths to success.[26] Positive geniuses recognize theirs is not the only vantage point and other interpretations of reality exist. Then they choose to believe or pursue the most valuable reality.

When I was in the ninth grade, I played on our school's basketball team. We were pretty good that year, and we made it to the state tournament. In fact, we made it to the third-place game, but we had a terrible first half. We were down by almost twenty points at halftime. By that point in the game, we were all very frustrated with each other, largely because I was a hard-headed and arrogant point guard. Our coach couldn't get us to stop arguing about who should be taking the most shots, and our star shooter had been shut down by their best defender. In the locker room at halftime, we all assumed the loss was inevitable and one of our best players left the locker room and quit on the spot, but that was actually the wake-up call we needed. Finally, our coach got through to us. With a speech worthy of a Hollywood blockbuster, he convinced us success was possible. With the confidence that resulted from the coach's encouragement, our star shooter started to make shots like we were used to him doing, and we won the game. The player who quit at halftime missed the celebration. Positive people see paths to success when negative people prematurely accept defeat.

Positivity and Semiotics

There is a common thread, with repeating themes, leading from creation into eternity. This thread tells a love story of restoration about a Father whose omniscience and passion for his children leads him to allow their discomfort. As I follow this thread through history and into the future, I am learning God has control of its path and pattern, and I am becoming more and more convinced there are good things to come down the road. The fear-based dispensational thinking that clouds the minds of a majority of Christians leads most to believe the thread leads to a dark destiny, but as I aim slightly west to hit the target in an eastern wind, I have begun to believe God gave us an affinity for happy endings to provoke optimism rather than fear. It is this optimism that gives us a wide-angle view to see the beautiful mosaic in which we find ourselves. This world is the canvas, and we are the paint that shines bright the beautiful plan of God. His story is not a map, a list, or even a description. It is a picture.

26. Achor, *Before Happiness*, 14.

One of the most important criteria of a successful world-changer is the ability to understand the world or read the signs of the times. Leonard Sweet says, "Disciples of Jesus must learn to read the sign-language of the Spirit."[27] If we are unable to read the signs of the times (see Matt 16:23), we will miss opportunities to join Jesus in his continuing mission. Pessimists either lack the ability or the desire to see or validate good potential. Their vision of the future is therefore obscured. Positive people are able to see both good and bad potential, and are energized by the pursuit of the good.

Beth Kuhel says, "Positive thinkers always see the big picture."[28] Pessimism and negative affect may actually cause Christians to fail to read the signs of the times. A study at the University of Toronto concluded that our mood can change how our eyes, more precisely our visual cortex, process information. In that experiment, individuals were made to feel either happy or sad, then they asked those individuals to look at a series of pictures. Those people who were made to feel sad failed to process many of the details of the images, but the individuals who were made to feel happy saw much more. This conclusion is similar to the conclusion of eye-tracking experiments. The positive emotions that test subjects experienced improved their ability to recognize details in a picture.[29]

For people who think negatively, the range of possible outcomes of a situation is limited. In her book *Positivity*, Barbara L. Fredrickson writes about her research that shows when the brain is negative, it operates in fight-or-flight mode, but when your brain is positive it can use its full range of intellectual, social, and emotional resources to recognize new ways of finding solutions.[30] "Thus a more positive employee is more likely to see avenues for job advancement in a company. A positive entrepreneur is able to see more open niches in the marketplace. A positive student is able to see more fellowships or scholarships to apply for. A positive athlete will see more players to pass to on the field, and so on."[31] Carmine Gallo writes, "optimists see the big picture" when other people are distracted by the way things are and the potential for things to get worse.[32]

---

27. Sweeney, "Leonard Sweet on Signs," para. 8.

28. Kuhel, "Positive People Attract," para. 17.

29. Schmitz, Rosa, and Anderson, "Opposing Influences," para. 9.

30. Fredrickson, *Positivity*, 62.

31. Achor, *Before Happiness*, 100.

32. Gallo, "5 Reasons Why Optimists," para. 6.

If we lack the ability to read the signs, we will not only fail to recognize how to participate in God's active work in the world, we will also lack the ability to communicate with the world. David Banks asserts "the church must make use of semiotically aware imagery to communicate how this message [that though we are broken, God, in his mercy and through Jesus Christ, offers to graciously put us back together again] is real for us."[33] But how will Christians do this if they are unable to see the signs because they are skeptical of the possibility of a church with a bright future?

It is through an image-rich communication of the gospel that Christians will successfully incarnate the good news of Jesus Christ to the world.[34] Images make the message powerful, memorable, and emotional. They connect us to the story, and that emotional connection is a primary key of lasting discipleship. Christine Mutch claims,

> in order for people to be transformed into the image of Christ in a deeply personal and sustainable way, practitioners must intentionally capitalize on the brain's emotional system, the powerful network which drives attention, memory, motivation, and decision-making, as well as one's ability to engage in transformational relationships with others and with God.[35]

A famous experiment performed by Christopher Chabris and Daniel Simons asked students to count the number of times a ball was passed in a game of catch. The students were so fixated on counting that about half of them completely failed to recognize a person dressed as a gorilla walked through the scene. In their book, Chabris and Simons write, "we vividly experience some aspects of our world, particularly those that are the focus of our attention. But this rich experience inevitably leads to the erroneous belief that we process all of the detailed information around us."[36] If an individual is watching for signs of decline and decay, he will see them, while failing to recognize the signs of improvement and health.

The part in the back of the eyeball that cannot absorb the light coming into the eye is the blind spot. There are always unknown areas in a person's reality, and each person can choose to assume the contents of those areas are good or bad. Pessimists assume the areas they can't see are filled with dangers, dead ends, disease, and failure. Irrational optimists choose

33. Banks, "Image of Grace," 7.

34. Sweet, *Giving Blood,* 52.

35. Mutch, "Sustainable Faith," 2.

36. Chabris and Simons, *Invisible Gorilla,* 7.

to believe blind spots are filled with ease, comfort, and predictability. "The positive genius fills in the blind spot with information that is true and valid and that leads to positive growth."[37]

Positive Psychology in Groups

Perhaps the most valuable news for the church about the productivity of positivity is the discoveries of positive psychology apply to the production of groups, not just of individuals. The principle that pleasant and unpleasant emotions fuel and deplete energy transfers almost indistinguishably from individuals to groups.[38] Groups whose emotions are mostly positive are more motivated, more creative, and harder working. They are better learners and more adaptable to the pace of change. They are more physically healthy, and they have better group cohesion and organizational commitment.[39] How do forward thinkers lead groups to positivity and set a tone of optimism? They make their own joy and optimism visible—and therefore contagious.

V. S. Ramachandran discovered the existence of mirror neurons, as documented in *The Neurons That Shaped Civilization*, when he discovered neurons in the frontal and parietal cortexes of macaque monkeys fire both when a monkey grabs something and when the monkey watches another monkey grab the same item.[40] Further research has shown these neurons exist in humans, and those neurons are not limited to the motor cortex.[41] What conclusion did that lead scientists to? It revealed the existence of emotional contagion. Individuals are constantly and involuntarily adopting the emotions of others. Paul told the church in Corinth that "bad company corrupts good character" (1 Cor 15:33 NLT). In addition, individuals mirror the emotions and actions of their leaders more strongly that they do other group members.

Tony Schwarz points out "the more you're able to move your attention to what makes you feel good, the more capacity you'll have to manage whatever was making you feel bad in the first place."[42] If this is true not only

---

37. Achor, *Before Happiness*, 57.
38. Humphrey, *Effective Leadership Theory*, 80.
39. Fredrickson, "Broaden-and-Build Theory," 1367–77.
40. Ramachandran, "Neurons That Shaped Civilization," 7:37.
41. Keysers et al., "Touching Sight," 335–46.
42. Schwartz, "Overcoming Your Negative Bias," para. 13.

about individuals but also about groups, that should give organizations the power to change the course of their businesses using positivity.

Pastors are frequently familiar with effective methods of tone-setting and vision-casting. Their tone of communication can come across as enthusiasm, motivation, and exhortation, or it can fall into the tempting tones of correction, warning, or even conspiracy theory. The balance of tone has shifted too often to the latter. A congregation inundated with negative potentials, alarmism, and fear-mongering will drift quickly toward negativity. The danger of this common habit of religious communication cannot be overstated. Not only will it lead individuals to unhealthy habits; it will also hinder their ability to be discipled and to serve as advocates for the Christian mission.

Leaders cannot force people to think positively, but they can instill positive realities into their thinking. Achor gives three strategies for transferring positivity to groups. They are: success franchising (coming up with a positive behavioral change that is easily replicated), script writing (changing a prevailing social script by making it positive), and creating shared narrative (creating value and meaning by appealing to emotion).[43]

Proverbs 13:20 says, "Walk with the wise and become wise, for a companion of fools suffers harm." Not only will these strategies introduce more positive people to the organization, but it is also far easier for an individual to sustain positivity when he or she is surrounded by positive people. Positivity is contagious in both directions. This does not mean the church should avoid disseminating negative feedback or facing undesirable realities, but it should avoid unnecessary negativity.

DISCUSSION QUESTIONS:

a. How can believing we have already arrived or accepting the way things are cause a person to become complacent?

b. When the widow in Luke 18 persistently asked the judge for justice, what gave her the confidence to keep asking even when she got turned down many times before?

c. As Christians, where should our confidence come from (Ps 59:9), and how can we move from doubt to confidence?

43. Achor, *Before Happiness*, 183.

d. Have you ever tried writing down things for which you are grateful each night before going to bed? If yes, how did it help you become a positive person?

e. In Colossians 3:23–24, when the apostle Paul told the Colossians to work confidently because they are guaranteed an inheritance from the Lord, what was the inheritance to which he was referring?

2

Positive Psychology Fuels Growth

It's always easier to follow someone with a positive outlook.[1]

—Victor Lipman

MANY PASTORS POSIT THEY would be happier if their church grew. Is it possible the inverse is true, that happiness could actually fuel the growth they believe God has called their church to experience? Barbara L. Fredrickson shows those individuals who are most positive are more creative, knowledgeable, resilient, socially integrated, and healthy, and these attributes lead those people to perform successfully.[2] Positivity level is a "key determinant" of the amount of energy individuals bring to their work,[3] and optimism is attractive and contagious. Positivity is also energizing, and the church is desperate for benefits of that mindset. This chapter will focus on the benefits that an increase in positivity offers the church. Positivity will actually help people in the church operate more productively in their role as disciple makers. The church is destined to grow, and it must not allow fear and pessimism to creep into its messaging.

I am currently the pastor of a growing church in Gillette, Wyoming called New Life Gillette Church. Our church is a member of The Wesleyan

---

1. Lipman, "Why A Positive Mindset," para. 5.
2. Fredrickson, "Broaden-and-Build Theory," 1367–77.
3. Ben-Shahar and Ridgway, Joy of Leadership, 78.

Church. Like most denominations, ours is divided into districts, and there are a few districts, including the one my church is in, that are exceptionally healthy. In a country that closes 4,000 Christian churches for every 1,000 it opens, our district is growing rapidly. Why is it growing? I believe it is largely a result of courage that comes from optimistic guidance.

The pastors of the churches in the Northwest District of The Wesleyan Church are backed by leaders (Isaac Smith, Wes Smith, and Wayne Mueller) who encourage them to take risks and believe success is possible, and the pastors in our district trust their leaders to support them when risks backfire. The joy and confidence that results from watching sister churches grow creates a healthy competition that motivates other churches to work harder. It also creates a feeling of optimism that church growth is possible, and it can be led by seemingly normal people. Church leaders here enjoy a healthy team environment that provides encouragement when setbacks happen, and there is collective celebration when success results. Pastors who have struggled to lead small churches in other districts have taken small churches in the Northwest District and led them to tremendous growth. There is no better example than the example of Pastor David Kinnan and Fountain Springs Church in Rapid City, South Dakota. David is an optimistic risk-taker who transformed a small but healthy church into one of the fastest-growing churches in America. His courage and innovation have encouraged many other pastors to pursue large-scale evangelism.

If all of the churches in America were placed on a scatter-plot diagram that shows the correlation between growth/decline rates and average attendance, annual giving, or the pastor's salary, you would begin to see trends in the data, but there would inevitably be outliers. The common scientific practice is to remove the outliers and focus on the trends. Tal Ben-Shahar calls this "the error of the average."[4] That's the first mistake traditional science makes. Shawn Achor says it this way: "If we study merely what is average, we will remain merely average."[5] It's time to start looking at the churches that buck the trend of decline and ask what they are doing right to reach people with the gospel while so many others fail to do so. Focus on the outliers like David Kinnan and Fountain Springs Church.

4. Ben-Shahar and Ridgway, *Joy of Leadership*, 78.

5. Achor, *Happiness Advantage*, 10.

PESSIMISM

The Christian church culture is suffering from excessive pessimism, believing the future will be worse than the past, and cynicism, believing pre-Christians are the enemy rather than the prize. Historically, America was seen as an optimistic country. The American Dream, although a flawed objective destined to result in disappointment, gave Americans hope, something to look forward to, but that seems to be rapidly changing. Pessimism and cynicism are gripping the nation on a large scale. Heather Long points out a surprising change in trend: 57 percent of Americans believe the country is "doing poorly," and 56 percent of Americans think the next generation will be worse off than they are financially, but is all this doom and gloom justified? No. Even though Americans are doing much better than they did in the past on multiple fronts, including finances, safety, and health,[6] ten times more people suffer from major depression now than in 1945.[7] Much of that depression is caused by an epidemic of pessimism. The good news is the church is best equipped to reverse that trend.

Causes of Pessimism

Social scientists have shown some individuals are wired with a disposition toward positivity. Some people are naturally more negative, but genetics only accounts for half (or less) of the factors that lead a person to be pessimistic or optimistic. No matter what their genetic predisposition, humans have the ability to express whichever psychology they choose.[8] We can overcome our genetic programming, and happiness is a state of mind that can be achieved.[9] We can choose to set our minds on things that are good and lovely, on things above or on things below. Happiness can be found even in dark times. In order to accomplish anything difficult in life, effort is required. Unfortunately, the church in America seems to believe a life of pessimism is the desirable option.

As a result of recent declines and poor eschatological considerations, the American church has abandoned long-game strategies to lead all people to a saving faith in Jesus Christ. The Christian church must choose

6. Long, "56 percent of Americans," para. 8.

7. Lane, *Loss of Happiness*, 22.

8. Lyubomirsky, *How of Happiness*, 24.

9. Lyubomirsky, *How of Happiness*, 24.

to adopt long-game strategies that optimistically seek to foster growth. In order to accomplish this, the American Christian church would be wise to put less trust in underdeveloped theologies that cause it to use short-game strategies to reach a few people in the days before the building collapses, and instead adopt long-game strategies that trust the building's foundation while they are used by God to reach many people.

Scheier and Carver prove "optimism confers benefits on what people do and what people are able to achieve in times of adversity."[10] They go on to say

> people's actions are greatly influenced by their expectations about the consequences of those actions. People who see desired outcomes as attainable continue to strive toward those outcomes, even when progress becomes difficult or slow. Alternatively, if outcomes seem sufficiently unattainable (regardless of the reason for the difficulty), people withdraw their effort and disengage themselves from the goals that they have set, even if the consequences of such disengagement are at times severe. Thus, we see people's expectancies as a major determinant of the disjunction between two general classes of behavior: continued striving vs. giving up and turning away.[11]

If "optimism is also correlated with measures of personality characteristics that are more positive in nature such as self-mastery, locus of control, and self-esteem,"[12] and happiness leads to success, why has the church failed to recognize this obvious contributing cause of numerical and influential decline?

Pessimism Doesn't Look Good

A University of Massachusetts study showed "positive affect tends to increase more when visual and auditory emotional information is congruent versus incongruent."[13] In this study, individuals were shown positive visual stimulation and negative visual stimulation, and the positive visual stimulation produced positive emotions. Pastor John Burke, author of *No Perfect People Allowed: Creating a Come as You are Culture in the Church*, wisely

10. Scheier and Carver, "Effects of Optimism," 202.
11. Scheier and Carver, "Effects of Optimism," 202.
12. Scheier and Carver, "Effects of Optimism," 215.
13. Leviyah et al.,, "Mood Changes," para. 9.

observes, "Generally, emerging generations do not ask, 'What is true?' They are primarily asking, 'Do I want to be like you?' They see truth as relational. If I want to be like you, then I want to consider what you believe. If I don't see anything real or attractive in you or your friends as Christ-followers, I don't care how 'true' you think it is. I'm not interested."[14] That's why what your parents believe played such a big role in helping you believe what you believe. If you had a good relationship with your parents, there is a very good chance you believe something very similar to what they believe. If you didn't have a good relationship with your parents, you will likely reject what they believe. Pessimism has a negative effect on the way the world sees the church. It's not attractive, and considering our primary objective to "make disciples of all nations," our pessimistic attitudes don't help.

Beth Kuhel says, "Positive people tend to be some of our biggest influencers in society and some of the world's most successful people. Their special charisma comes from how they react to difficulty and challenges and how they use every experience as a stepping-stone toward a better future."[15] This obvious fact should lead us to adopt a positive tone in order to more effectively influence society. This is not to say we should adopt a fantasy Christianity that claims following Christ will only result in easy living and incessant positive emotions, but optimism for the future of Christianity will attract people.

We have been brainwashed to believe goodness is decreasing, but that is demonstrably false. The arguments and proofs pessimists use to show declines are reliant on the communication technologies that have made atrocities and disasters appear to occur more frequently than in the past when wrongdoing and tragedy occurred without recognition. Maybe Christians should watch less cable news. Twenty-four/seven news begs for conflict and disaster. Steven Pinker writes,

> Whether or not the world really is getting worse, the nature of news will interact with the nature of cognition to make us think that it is. News is about things that happen, not things that don't happen. We never see a journalist saying to the camera, "I'm reporting live from a country where a war has not broken out"—or a city that has not been bombed, or a school that has not been shot up. As long as bad things have not vanished from the face of the earth, there will always be enough incidents to fill the news,

14. Burke, *No Perfect People Allowed*, 42–43.

15. Kuhel, "Positive People Attract," para. 1.

especially when billions of smartphones turn most of the world's population into crime reporters and war correspondents.[16]

In 1999, many of the families in the small church our family attended heard rumors of a computer bug that would cause computers all over the world to crash. The theory speculated that these crashes would lead to nuclear fallout, food and water shortages, economic collapse, and mass hysteria. Our family stocked food and water, helped to spread fearful rumors, and withdrew the little cash we had from the bank. That week my mom's purse was stolen with all my money in it. They called the theory Y2K. It came and went. Our computers were fine, but my money was gone. Computer programmers assured the public the conspiracy theories were overstated, but we doubted their analysis and prepared for the worst-case scenario. For a few months, we were preppers, and I was left with no money.

We are naturally drawn to fear. Every day, we experience triggers that prompt negativity and push us into the fight-or-flight mode. These triggers are like bees landing on us. Because of our natural defense mechanisms, we can't help but think about the bee. Sometimes we can just swat the triggers away, but other times they sting us. When that happens, the pain is all we can think about. Positive things can also trigger us. We can be positively triggered by a loved one, a beautiful picture, or a song, but positive triggers don't grab our attention as easily as negative triggers. Usually, we have to go out of our way to give attention to a positive trigger, but negative triggers grab our attention.

Tara Westover's autobiography, *Educated*, was one of the bestselling books of 2018. Hordes of people have been captivated by this story of a father whose conspiracy theories and apocalyptic predictions caused his family to live in seclusion. Tara's father, Val Westover, is a survivalist and a prepper, and his extreme Mormon beliefs cause him to reject modern medicine and education. His conspiracies have survived decades of human advancement because he refuses to acknowledge the world is improving and immorality is decreasing.

It's difficult to trust a sinking ship, but we keep telling the world that's what the church is. When Jesus rebuked the storm in Mark 4, he asked his disciples, "Why are you so afraid? Do you still have no faith?" (Mark 4:40). Then the disciples were astonished and said, "Who is this? Even the wind and the waves obey him" (Mark 4:41). If the wind and waves obey him and

---

16. Pinker, *Enlightenment Now*, 41.

this world cannot overcome him, how can we doubt the resilience and effectiveness of his body, his bride, the church?

Firefighters and Pastors

With so many fires, line-of-duty deaths, and other critical incidents, in addition to the wear and tear of daily life, the firefighting profession is among the most stressful jobs there is. It is widely believed firefighters are at a greater risk of developing mental health difficulties, and firefighters commit suicide at a higher rate than the rest of society. Colleen Martin argues these factors interfere with firefighters' ability to have healthy relationships, perform their jobs, and take care of themselves.[17] It can be argued the life of a pastor is similar to the life of a firefighter. Although the suicide rate of the pastors is below the average of the societies in which they reside, presumably due to a biblical foundation, the stresses of the pastorate are significant. This stress is compounded by the dominant belief that it is the pastor's job to express God's displeasure with society and the imminent demolition of the world.

In light of the evidence of the benefits of positivity, the depressing culture in which clergy operate will not help them reach their full potential to reach as many people as possible with the good news of Jesus Christ. One might argue finding ways to make the occupation less depressing is watering down the calling, but maybe that line of reasoning is what is causing the struggles of the dispensational church. Negativity repels. Perhaps that is why half of all employees leave their job to get away from their manager.[18] The large number of clergy who leave the pastorate every month were not able to rely solely on a biblical foundation as a source of excitement for the mission.

In an excellent direction for pastors, John Piper writes,

> Whatever measure of pessimism a pastor may feel or I may feel about our own society as Christians, we should be long-term optimists. And I think premillennialists and amillennialists can say this with as much or more confidence than postmillennialists, though everybody can say it in those three camps. Sooner or later Christ is, in fact, going to break into this world and put everything right. He is going to cast the weeds into outer darkness, and he is

17. Buser et al., "Depression & PTSD," para. 1.
18. Robins, "8 Reasons Why," para. 45.

going to establish his kingdom, and the world will be full of the glory of the Lord like the waters cover the sea, and righteousness and justice and peace will kiss all for the glory of Christ. That is coming and we should be deeply, deeply confident and optimistic about it.[19]

For the sake of the kingdom, and for their own sake, Pastors should be long-term optimists.

BIBLICAL OPTIMISM

When I talk about biblical optimism, I am not talking about blind optimism, and I am not talking about emotional happiness. There are two types of optimism: unrealistic/blind optimism and realistic optimism. When I use the phrase "biblical optimism," I'm referring to the latter type, realistic optimism. Jim Collins, in his famous book *Good to Great*, gives optimism a bad name by his explanation of the Stockdale Paradox.[20] In his telling of the story of Vietnam prisoners who were overly optimistic about the timeline of their release, Collins points out those soldiers who believed they would be released by a specific time eventually gave up hope. Biblical optimism is more like the hope found in the prison movie *The Shawshank Redemption*: "I'll keep an eye out for you and the chessboard ready. Remember Red, hope is a good thing. Maybe the best of things, and no good thing ever dies. I will be hoping that this letter finds you and finds you well."[21]

I'm not endorsing blind optimism for the Christian church or pointing to unrealistic timelines. I'm arguing for optimism that is well-founded in the truth of biblical prophecy, the experienced faithfulness of God, and the hope that is built on nothing less than Jesus' blood and righteousness. This optimism can be compared to Christian faith. We aren't confident in ourselves. We are confident in our leader, and our faith in him has no expiration date. "Faith is confidence in what we hope for and assurance about what we do not see" (Heb 11:1).

Biblical optimism is hope and faith in God. It trusts that God has a plan and that he is powerful enough to accomplish it. When Haman planned to kill the Jews, Mordecai appealed to Esther to stand up for the people of Israel with one of the most iconic challenges in history, "perhaps

19. Piper, "Gospel Hope," para. 6.

20. Collins, *Good to Great*, 83.

21. Darabont, *Shawshank Redemption*.

you were made queen for just such a time as this?," but he preceded his challenge with an optimistic statement about the sovereignty of God, "If you keep quiet at a time like this, deliverance and relief for the Jews will arise from some other place" (Esth 4:14). Mordecai knew it was possible for Esther to falter, but he also knew God would not. Christian optimism is not an emotion; it is a decision to respond to hard circumstances with hope for the future. It trusts in the sovereignty of God.

Positivity and Persecution

Luke 19 documents a parable Jesus told about a nobleman and his ten servants. The "nobleman was called away to a distant empire to be crowned king and then return. Before he left, he called together ten of his servants and divided among them ten pounds of silver, saying, 'Invest this for me while I am gone.' But his people hated him and sent a delegation after him to say, 'We do not want him to be our king'" (Luke 19:12–14). Apparently, Christians, like these ten servants, are called to serve God productively even when the people around us despise our Master. In addition to facing the normal challenges associated with leading people, we will often have to face the challenge of working in an environment that is hostile to our Master. Someday our master will return to Earth, and in the meantime, we are commanded to turn a profit, to achieve our missional goal. Complaining and giving excuses to the Master won't get the job done. In those times relentless optimism is crucial.

God, the maker of our bodies, and therefore our brains, speaks through King David when he says, "Take delight in the Lord, and he will give you the desires of your heart" (Ps 37:4). David connected delight and achievement in that order, knowing delight usually comes before accomplishment. "Theologians and scientists alike are beginning to understand the important intersection of spiritual formation and brain research."[22] Making a connection between delight, or positivity, and success is not a new construct. The apostle Paul also seems to tap into the benefits of optimism. He writes to the Corinthians, "That is why, for Christ's sake, I delight in weaknesses, in insults, in hardships, in persecutions, in difficulties. For when I am weak, then I am strong. I have made a fool of myself, but you drove me to it. I ought to have been commended by you, for I am not in the least inferior to the 'super-apostles,' even though I am nothing" (2 Cor

22. Mutch, "Sustainable Faith," 13.

12:10–11). Even when the future seemed grim to the world, Paul was able to see the glorious future God had in store.

Perhaps it was the positivity of Christians that caused persecution to advance and rejuvenate the followers of Christ. Acts 8:18 shows some of the original success of evangelism came as a result of persecution. As the church was persecuted, they spread out geographically, taking the gospel with them. In Luke 21:12–13, Jesus warns his disciples of persecution, but he also encourages his audience that persecution will create an opportunity for evangelism.

When following Christ becomes a hobby or a means for personal or financial gain, complacency causes Christians to lack urgency and fail to prioritize evangelism. Sometimes pain and persecution clarify priorities and remove distractions, but comfort causes confusion. A few years after a failed attempt at planting a church after college, my motivations turned from sacrificing for the advancement of the kingdom as a church planter to using my religious education to gain financial stability for my family. I decided the inability of small churches to provide a reasonable salary and accomplish simple ministry goals meant if I were going to work in a church, it should be a large church. So, I interviewed for a job at a megachurch in Oklahoma City that had helped renew my belief in the local church, LifeChurch.tv. On April 1, 2009, they offered me the job via email, but the salary they offered was much less than I wanted it to be. That salary would not provide the financial stability I had prioritized in my search for a job. I forwarded the email to my wife with this message: "Welp, it looks like I won't be working at LifeChurch," but after sending the email I realized I didn't forward the email to my wife. I had responded to the pastor of the church with that short, arrogant message. To cover my tracks, I had a brilliant idea and sent a follow up email that said, "April fools! I'll get back to you soon about the position." It won't surprise you to hear that, although we attended and volunteered at LifeChurch.tv for a few years, I never had a paying job there.

The disappointment I experienced as a result of the failed church plant does not qualify as persecution, but the frustration I experienced caused me to be cynical of the value of the local church and to be selfish in my desire to participate in the local church. The motivation to sacrifice for the Christian mission must come from a place other than comfort. The Christian's hope does not come from constant success, but from knowing God and his sovereignty. The joy of the Lord is their strength (Neh 8:10).

His power gives optimism and hope for the future that goes beyond logical understanding.

Jeremiah 29:11 says, "'For I know the plans I have for you,' declares the Lord, 'plans to prosper you and not to harm you, plans to give you hope and a future.'" Contrary to popular belief, neither Jeremiah 29:11 nor any other passage in Scripture, promises that following Christ will be easy. In fact, Jeremiah 29:11 is not even written to Christians. It is written to the Jews to encourage them to be long-term optimists, but even then they would have to wait seventy years for the plans to be accomplished. Our hope is not found in an expectation of personal gain or even in personal happiness; it is found in faith in God, who has a long-term plan.

When his builders were tempted to give up, Nehemiah held a church service and delivered an uplifting message of hope and strength that comes from the joy of the Lord:

> Then Nehemiah the governor, Ezra the priest and teacher of the Law, and the Levites who were instructing the people said to them all, "This day is holy to the Lord your God. Do not mourn or weep." For all the people had been weeping as they listened to the words of the Law. Nehemiah said, "Go and enjoy choice food and sweet drinks, and send some to those who have nothing prepared. This day is holy to our Lord. Do not grieve, for the joy of the Lord is your strength." (Neh. 8:5)

Justification for Optimism

Marian Tupy writes,

> Over the last 200 years or so, the world has experienced previously unimaginable improvements in standards of living. The process of rapid economic growth started in Europe and America, but today some of the world's fastest-growing countries can be found in Asia and Africa—lifting billions of people from absolute poverty. Historical evidence, therefore, makes a potent case for optimism.[23]

If you believe God cares for the poor, widows, and the least of these, you have to believe we live in the best time since Adam and Eve walked the earth. This does not mean there is nothing wrong with the world as it is today or that it does not have a lot of improving to do, but it does mean

23. Tupy, "Things are Getting Better," para. 3.

improvement has been somewhat consistent throughout history. Hans Rosling writes, "Over the past twenty years, the proportion of the global population living in extreme poverty has halved."[24] For those Christians who made it through the COVID-19 pandemic and simply had to stay home, it feels like we made it through the apocalypse, and the apocalypse was a lot more comfortable than they thought it would be. Some will point to COVID-19 as evidence that fear is warranted. Others will point to it as evidence that we can manage more today than we ever could have managed in the past. Steven Pinker, the Johnstone Professor of Psychology at Harvard University, writes,

> The world has made spectacular progress in every single measure of human well-being . . . Problems are inevitable, because our knowledge will always be infinitely far from complete. Some problems are hard, but it is a mistake to confuse hard problems with problems unlikely to be solved. Problems are soluble, and each particular evil is a problem that can be solved. An optimistic civilization is open and not afraid to innovate, and is based on traditions of criticism. Its institutions keep improving, and the most important knowledge that they embody is knowledge of how to detect and eliminate errors.[25]

There is, however, some disagreement about the exact amount of progress in one primary area: freedom, especially religious freedom. It is true that at least since 2008, the world has "witnessed a sustained attack on political and economic freedoms, as well as freedoms of religion and free expression," but in order to get a complete picture of the history of religious freedom, a look at a time period greater than a decade is necessary.[26] Setbacks must not be seen as long-term declines. In the Common Era, one of "the world's first official declaration[s] of universal religious freedom" did not come about until emperor Constantine joined emperor Licinius in issuing the Edict of Milan in 313, and the phrase "religious liberty" wasn't coined until Tertullian used it in AD 197.[27] Since that time, the world has seen a steady (not constant) increase in religious liberty, and where religious liberty increases, all of human prosperity increases.[28]

24. Rosling, *Factfulness*, 6.

25. Pinker, *Enlightenment Now*, 52.

26. Tupy, "Update on the Global State," para. 4.

27. Wolterstorff, "Story about Religious Freedom," para. 19.

28. Gill, "Religious Liberty," 116.

For most of human history, a nation's progress on freedom and liberty were not considered a subject of international concern. Before World War II, "massacres of ethnic groups within a country were met with little more than polite statements of disapproval. Less flagrant violations were not even considered a fit subject for diplomatic conversation."[29] Now, governments at all levels at least proclaim their commitment to human rights. When freedom of religion was enshrined in the Bill of Rights, nearly the entire world began to recognize the value of religious freedom.[30]

This does not mean progress is inevitable, but it gives reason for biblical optimism. Because human progress is not linear, the timeline of progress over recorded history moves up and to the right, but temporary setbacks lead some people to fear the worst rather than expect the continuation of progress.[31] When you consider the long timeline rather than snapshots in history, freedom is rising, including religious freedom, but even if the world had not seen such an increase in religious freedom, the American Christian church would not have legitimate cause for concern. It is undeniable that the world now exercises religious freedom at a much higher rate than was experienced when the church was founded, and that did not stifle growth for the early church.[32] In fact, persecution often caused growth (Acts 8:4).

It is time for Christians to point more often to successes, to advancement, to peace, to the decline of poverty, to the growth of the church, and to the advancement of freedom that is all around us. Tupy writes,

> An average person today is much better off than he or she would have been at any previous period in human history. That's obviously true of citizens of developed nations, who are the beneficiaries of two hundred years of material, scientific, technological and medical progress. But that's also true of ordinary people in the developing countries, who have seen tremendous improvements in their standards of living since the end of World War II.[33]

29. Malamud, *Human Rights in Brief*, 5.
30. Malamud, *Human Rights in Brief*, 17.
31. "What We Do," para. 22.
32. Schirrmacher, "Persecution and Mission," para. 1.
33. Tupy, "Hollywood's Apocalypse Obsession Ignores Reality," para. 3.

Humanity is winning the war on famine[34] and poverty.[35] Violence and war are becoming rarer,[36] and freedom is expanding.[37] Knowledge is increasing at a staggering rate.[38] Crime is plummeting,[39] and legal slavery has all but disappeared.[40] Racism and sexism are declining,[41] and the best news is the church is growing.[42]

When COVID-19 struck America, it seemed many of the same people who bragged about being prepared for the apocalypse with basements full of food, water, and ammunition were the same people who had become so used to comfort and convenience that they loudly complained when Cracker Barrel didn't open early enough. The common Christian refrain when the world experiences widespread pain or change is "Jesus is coming soon," "this is definitely the last days," or worst of all, "Jesus, come get us."[43] The pessimism and selfishness that are reveled in the desire to be removed from the world, like Jonah, rather than stay in it to show God's love to as many people as possible are evidence of our judgmental, bunkering mentality.[44] The reality is even painful changes almost always lead to improvement and growth. COVID-19 and the Black Lives Matter protests of 2020 exercised muscles that would have otherwise become frail. Economic downturns usually lead to innovation and frugality, and even persecution leads to church growth.

A Look Ahead

If you were drawn to this book because of the provocative title about the *Left Behind* series and are wondering when I am going to address the books, that will come in chapter 5, but I believe it is important for us to set a foundation by talking about what is at stake. When I began to believe the church was

34. Tupy, "How Humanity Won," para. 1.

35. Wang, "Poverty in Numbers," para. 2.

36. Pinker, *Better Angels of Our Nature*, 190.

37. Tupy, "Hong Kong and the Power of Economic Freedom," 187.

38. Pinker, *Enlightenment Now*, 7.

39. Pinker, *Better Angels of Our Nature*, 1.

40. Tupy, "Is Moral Progress Real?," para. 1.

41. Aziz, "Less Racism and Sexism," para. 11.

42. Jenkins, *Next Christendom*, 2, 263.

43. Moore, "Jesus, Come Get Us."

44. See Jonah 1:13.

not the best method of Christian advancement, I abandoned the bride of Christ. When athletes believe a game is lost, effort wanes. When firefighters believe a burning house is a lost cause, they stop fighting for the house and turn to containment. If we have plenty of reason to be optimistic, but we choose to be pessimistic, we are causing our own failure. The next chapter will show that pessimism, cynicism, and judgmentalism have earned the church an image problem that is causing much of that failure.

DISCUSSION QUESTIONS:

a. What can Christians do to make the church more irresistible to outsiders?

b. How does a person find comfort in realistic optimism without falling for blind, pie-in-the sky optimism?

c. Why do the negative things that happen in the world get more attention than the positive things?

3

The Church's Image Problem

We, as the church, need to admit we don't look that good. When others see us, they're not all that attracted to us and wonder why we don't make some changes.[1]

—THOM AND JOANI SHULTZ

THE AMERICAN CHURCH IS FALLING BEHIND

THE CHURCH IS NOT dying. In fact, Philip Jenkins, in *The Next Christendom*, argues Christianity "should enjoy a worldwide boom in the coming decades," and even in America, "Christianity is very much alive and well."[2] The growth of Christianity in the United States however is not quite keeping pace with the growth of the population of the United States, but that is largely because nominal Christians are becoming convictional Christians or leaving the church. Ed Stetzer writes, "the percentage of convictional Christians in the US population has remained generally stable. What have changed are the numbers and beliefs of cultural and congregational Christians. As a result of the collapse of mainline Protestantism and the growth

1. Schultz, *Why Nobody Wants*, 254.
2. Jenkins, *Next Christendom*, 2, 263.

of secularism, convictional Christianity has incrementally moved outside the American cultural mainstream."[3] A 2012 study from the Pew Forum on Religion and Public Life states, "One-fifth of the U.S. public—and a third of adults under 30—are religiously unaffiliated."[4] In a 2015 report called "American's Changing Religious Landscape," Pew notes, "The Christian share of the U.S. population is declining, while the number of U.S. adults who do not identify with any organized religion is growing."[5] That Pew report shows that "those with no religious affiliation, or the 'nones,' were increasing at a faster rate than ever before,"[6] and from 2007 to 2014, the number of people who categorized themselves as unaffiliated grew from 16.1 percent to 22.8 percent.[7] *USA Today* reports "there is an eleven percent decrease in those who call themselves Christian. It shows the biggest growth factor occurring in those who say they have 'no religion.'"[8] Even Gallup, whose research appears to be the most optimistic about the number of people who attend church on a regular basis, admits the American church is not growing as fast as the population.[9]

Resistible Church

David Kinnaman and Gabe Lyons attribute this struggle of the Christian church in America to Christianity's "image problem."[10] In fact, the perception of Christians is so bad that in many circles simply carrying the "Christian" brand labels a person "irrelevant" or even an "extremist."[11] Positivity and optimism for church growth will help the church reverse the negative opinion that outsiders have of the church. The very cynicism and pessimism that feed the church's image problem are also at the heart of its failure to find solutions, and it shouldn't be surprising that the unfavorable opinions of people disconnected from the church have translated into problems in the church. Forty-two percent of Americans believe "people of faith" are

3. Stetzer, *Christians in the Age of Outrage*, 9.

4. Lugo, "'Nones' on the Rise," para. 1.

5. Pew Research Center, "America's Changing Religious Landscape," para. 1.

6. Murphy, "Missional Communities," 8.

7. Pew Research Center, "America's Changing Religious Landscape," para. 2.

8. Grossman, "Most Religious Groups," para. 8.

9. Shattuck, "7 Startling Facts," para. 1.

10. Kinnaman and Lyons, *Unchristian*, 84.

11. Kinnaman and Lyons, *Good Faith*, 21.

part of the problem when it comes to what happens in the country today, and even more, 46 percent, say "religion" is part of the problem.[12] Christians have been ruled out by many when it comes to finding solutions to the nation's problems. "Today only one-fifth of U.S. adults strongly believe that clergy are a credible source of wisdom and insight when it comes to the most important issues of our day."[13] Pre-Christians don't necessarily have a problem with pastors or priests, but they don't see the insights of clergy as "relevant to living real life."[14] Many pre-Christians are not aware that some of the "essential instructions of our society emerged from the Christian worldview."[15]

Kinnaman (a researcher for the Barna Group) and Lyons spent two years researching and conducting thousands of interviews to determine the cause of the image problem behind the decline in Christian church participation in the United States. According to their research, many of those outside of Christianity, especially younger adults, have little trust in the Christian faith, and esteem for the lifestyle of Christ-followers is quickly fading among pre-Christians. They admit their emotional and intellectual barriers go up when they are around Christians, and they reject Jesus because they feel rejected by Christians.[16]

It is tempting to ignore the intensity with which the younger generations hold these views, but, considering its calling to actively engage the ideas of culture in order to win them for Christ, the church must take it upon itself to understand their perspectives. What has the church done to cause young people to feel rejected by Christians? Pre-Christians "think the church no longer represents what Jesus had in mind, that Christianity in our society is not what it was meant to be,"[17] and Christians should learn to sympathize with the conclusions of pre-Christians rather than cynically condemn their opinions. Too often, Christians send repelling messages with their judgmentalism, cynicism, and pessimism. Pessimism about the likelihood of influencing a change in a person's life or cynicism about that person's desire to discover truth causes some Christians to view pre-Christians with disdain rather than with care and hope.

---

12. Kinnaman and Lyons, *Good Faith*, 13.

13. Kinnaman and Lyons, *Good Faith*, 13.

14. Kinnaman and Lyons, *Good Faith*, 29.

15. Kinnaman and Lyons, *Good Faith*, 33.

16. Schultz, *Why Nobody Wants*, 90.

17. Schultz, *Why Nobody Wants*, 161.

Engaging Communication

The current struggles of the American church have been intensified by its failure to communicate effectively. The church's inability to reach the youngest generation is not only a result of the generation's resistance to organized religion. It is also due to the church's inability to speak with a positive tone.[18] "The missional community is to incarnate the kingdom of God into the particular context in which God has called them."[19] In *Viral: How Social Media is Poised to Ignite Revival*, Leonard Sweet writes, "The primary missional challenge of the church will be to incarnate the gospel in a Google world."[20] This challenge is compounded by the complexity of the Google culture. As communication technology expands, the number of subcultures increases, leading to more communication barriers, and as Alan Hirsch points out, communication barriers make it more difficult to communicate the gospel message.[21] In addition, within each subculture are people in various stages of readiness to hear the gospel. The church is challenged to share its faith with pre-Christians of all kinds: with uninterested individuals (agnostics), interested faith shoppers (including the effort to compete with non-Christian faiths), and skeptics who aggressively object to the gift Christians offer pre-Christians.

Kinnaman and Lyons say, "The primary reason outsiders[22] feel hostile toward Christians, and especially conservative Christians, is . . . our 'swagger,' how we go about things and the sense of self-importance we project."[23] In their exploration of thousands of outsiders' impressions, they discovered "Christians are primarily perceived for what they stand against. [They] have become famous for what [they] oppose, rather than what [they] are for."[24] The church's cynical attitude about the behavior of pre-Christians causes its communication to be perceived primarily as judgmental. Pre-Christians believe Christians don't like them because of "what they do, how they look,

18. Kinnaman, *You Lost Me*, 39.

19. Murphy, "Missional Communities," 14.

20. Sweet, *Viral*, 10.

21. Hirsch, "Missional Velocity."

22. David Kannaman and Gabe Lyons use the word "outsider" to refer to atheists, agnostics, those of a faith other than Christianity, unchurched individuals with no firm religious convictions, and unchurched individuals who claim to believe in God. This book will use the words "outsider" and "pre-Christian" somewhat interchangably.

23. Kinnaman and Lyons, *Unchristian*, 26.

24. Kinnaman and Lyons, *Unchristian*, 26.

or what they believe. They feel minimized—or worse, demonized—by those who love Jesus."[25] That Google world Sweet writes about will not hear us unless we alter their perception of us.

The three most common perceptions of present-day Christianity are antihomosexual (an image held by 91 percent of young outsiders), judgmental (87 percent), and hypocritical (85 percent). These "big three" are followed by the following negative perceptions, embraced by a majority of young adults: "old-fashioned, too involved in politics, out of touch with reality, insensitive to others, boring, not accepting of other faiths, and confusing."[26] That survey was completed over ten years ago, and in *Good Faith*, Kinnaman and Lyons point out that perceptions of those surveyed over ten years ago "were a prediction of the crisis today."[27]

The antihomosexual conversation is of primary importance to the youngest generations, and the church must take much care in its response. The homophobic language of many Christians and the delayed response to the LGBT question by others has caused divisions within the church and between the church and pre-Christians. Too often, same-sex attraction and gay sex have been lumped together, causing unnecessary confusion and pain.[28] Same-sex attraction has been treated as a sin rather than a cause for compassion and an opportunity for discipleship. This is a conversation the church has to get right.

The numbers get even more discouraging when a person considers children within the church. Young adults who regularly attend church hold these same negative perceptions of the church. "Four out of five young churchgoers say that Christianity is antihomosexual; half describe it as judgmental, too involved in politics, hypocritical, and confusing; one-third believe their faith is old-fashioned and out of touch with reality; and one-quarter of young Christians believe it is boring and insensitive to others."[29]

These perceptions are the results of an overemphasis on truth rather than a healthy balance of grace and truth. Christ came from the Father "full of grace and truth" (John 1:14). Young pre-Christians are looking for Christians who reflect the gracious fruits of the spirit, not Christians who look first to judge outsiders. It is time for the church to stop defending its

25. Kinnaman and Lyons, *Unchristian*, 28.

26. Kinnaman and Lyons, *Unchristian*, 28.

27. Kinnaman and Lyons, *Good Faith*, 169.

28. Kinnaman and Lyons, *Good Faith*, 170.

29. Kinnaman and Lyons, *Unchristian*, 34.

way of communicating the gospel message and accept that it has earned these negative perceptions.

In *unChristian*, Kinnaman and Lyons write, "Nearly two out of every five young outsiders (38 percent) claim to have a 'bad impression of present-day Christianity.'"[30] They discovered that "One-third of young outsiders said that Christianity represents a negative image with which they would not want to be associated,"[31] and these perceptions of outsiders are now affecting the actions and ideas of young insiders. Young Christians

> are reluctant to admit they are Christians. They don't fear being unpopular, but they feel that raising the Christian flag would actually undermine their ability to connect with people and to maintain credibility with them. This is a major indictment of unChristian faith, that to bring those around them closer to Christ, they must distance themselves from the current "branding" of Christianity.[32]

Part of the problem is "a generation of young Christians believes that the churches in which they were raised are not safe and hospitable places to express doubts."[33] Why, then, would they trust the church to treat pre-Christians with hospitality? They have heard the clichéd talking points of the older generations to their honest questions. Those clichés appear to be inauthentic and very hostile to millennials and Generation Z. American teens are among the most religiously active Americans, but "American twentysomethings are the least religiously active."[34] They are not only leaving because they were not discipled correctly. They are also leaving because they don't want to be associated with the church. They are not necessarily walking away from faith, but they are walking away from the church.[35]

Although young Christians may be ashamed of the reputation of the church, they are not ashamed of Jesus. Therefore, a quality rebranding would bring energy to the church. It would help the church reach young pre-Christians, reengage with young people who have left the church, and retain the young believers still connected to the church. There are

30. Kinnaman and Lyons, *Unchristian*, 24.

31. Kinnaman and Lyons, *Unchristian*, 24.

32. Kinnaman and Lyons, *Unchristian*, 35.

33. Kinnaman, *You Lost Me*, 11.

34. Kinnaman, *You Lost Me*, 22.

35. Kinnaman, *You Lost Me*, 26.

thousands of Christian young people in America who want "nothing more than to elevate the relevance of Jesus to our culture."[36]

A contributor to this problem is found in the common belief among Christians that there has been a dramatic increase in human sinfulness, and that sinfulness is evidence Christ will soon return.[37] This belief has caused many to interpret the resistance of pre-Christians as an inevitable next step in the fulfillment of prophecy, rather than a problem that needs to be corrected. If pre-Christians are resistant, they are too often discarded as unchosen by advocates of election and declared stuck in their sin by others. Rather than love relentlessly and offer Christlike hospitality, those Christians are quick to label a skeptic or a prodigal as a lost cause. This mentality has become recognizable to pre-Christians and translates into resistance and complaints about hypocrisy and judgmentalism.

ANALYZING THE DATA

Understanding the Numbers

In interpreting the cause of the decline of the share of Americans who call themselves Christian, there are some statistical illusions to consider. The growth of some large churches may skew the numbers of church attendance.[38] It is not a coincidence the states whose church attendance is coming closest to keeping pace with population growth are the states with some of the largest churches in the country: Hawaii, Arkansas, Oklahoma, South Carolina, and Tennessee.[39]

The fact that people who attend a megachurch are less likely to attend on an every-week basis may also skew attendance numbers. If people attend less often, the average total attendance may decline while the number of people who attend on a fairly regular basis might stay the same or even increase. This problem is compounded by the reality that most churches do not take attendance. Most churches rely on a head count rather than

---

36. Kinnaman and Lyons, *Unchristian*, 35.

37. Altrogge, "What is This World Coming to?," para. 14.

38. Smietana, "Statistical Illusion," para. 11.

39. Shattuck, "7 Startling Facts," para. 27.

tracking the frequency of an individual's attendance. How can we know how many different people attend our church if we don't take attendance?

In other cases, the problem may be worse than it appears because many individuals claim to attend church more often than they actually do, and many people claim to go to church who actually do not. The "National Congregations Study" calls this the "the halo effect."[40] The halo effect is the difference between what people tell pollsters and what people actually do. Kelly Shattuck points out "Americans tend to overreport socially desirable behavior like voting and attending church and underreport socially undesirable behavior like drinking."[41] As church attendance becomes less socially desirable, reports of church attendance will decrease even if actual attendance does not.

With these statistical considerations in mind, it is still obvious much of the church's evangelistic struggles are due to an exodus of the younger generations from regular church attendance, but there is also another group of individuals leaving the church, those individuals who are not leaving *faith* in Jesus Christ but who have determined the church is not the best place to learn, fellowship, and worship. For these people, podcasts, online church, social media, and the growing worship music industry have served as a church replacement. A Barna study showed "eighty-eight percent of adults say their faith is important to them, but most choose not to grow their faith in church."[42] And when you consider the importance of church to churchgoers, "nearly two-thirds (64 percent) of people in the United States are open to pursuing their faith in an environment that's different from a typical church."[43]

The Well Curve

A caveat is warranted in this discussion. It is true that overall church participation percentages in America are declining, but a few studies may give reason for optimism within the statistics. A 2017 Harvard Study shows the decline in religious affiliation in America can be attributed to the secularization of the people who were "moderately religious."[44] In other words,

40. Chaves et al., "National Congregations Study," 6.
41. Shattuck, "7 Startling Facts," para. 8.
42. Barna Group, "Americans are Exploring," para. 4.
43. Barna Group, "Americans are Exploring," para. 10.
44. Schnabel and Bock, "Persistent and Exceptional Intensity," 686.

many of those people who are "lukewarm" have been compelled to leave the church (Rev 3:15–17). The people who in the past claimed "no strong affiliation" have begun to claim "no affiliation," but the percent of people who claim "strong affiliation" has actually increased over the past 35 years.[45]

In 2008, Leonard Sweet, in his book *Aqua Church 2.0*, used futur-eminded semiotics to see that the "normal distribution curve" is no longer a "bell curve" but a "well curve."[46] A well curve is a graph with the opposite shape of a bell curve. Chad Hall points out that televisions are simultaneously getting larger (flat-screen televisions) and smaller (cell phones). Stores are getting larger (superstores) and smaller (boutiques). People are eating more healthy food (Whole Foods) and more fast food (Chick-Fil-A).[47] Whether you look at politics, business, or the church, people are fleeing the middle ground, and, in order to minister to this world, the church must take ministry "to the edges, not to the center" where the best-of-both-world solutions are.[48] The thriving churches are the smallest and largest churches, and the dedicated are becoming more dedicated as the less-dedicated leave. The moderate church is disappearing.

Looking South

There are some reasons for concern for Christianity in America, but the growth of Christianity in the Global South could be the best news to Christian growth advocates. Timothy C. Tennent says "the church is experiencing unprecedented growth outside the West, far away from the traditional centers of theological reflection."[49] Philip Jenkins, in *The Next Christendom: The Coming of Global Christianity*, argues that "until recently, the overwhelming majority of Christians have lived in White nations," making it appear to be the religion of the haves.[50] Recently, though, the numbers have shifted. The largest Christian communities are now in the south. "The center of gravity in the Christian world has shifted inexorably southward, to Africa, Asia, and Latin America."[51] If Christians even maintain their current share

45. Schnabel and Bock, "Persistent and Exceptional Intensity," 688.

46. Sweet, *AquaChurch 2.0*, 173.

47. Hall, "Leader's Insight," para. 4.

48. Sweet, *AquaChurch 2.0*, 174.

49. Tennent, *Theology in the Context of World Christianity*, 193.

50. Jenkins, *Next Christendom*, 2.

51. Jenkins, *Next Christendom*, 2.

of the populations of the southern countries, the number of Christians in the world will soon drastically increase because those countries are growing at such a rapid rate. The skin color of the average Christian is getting darker, and Christianity is becoming more Pentecostal and traditional.[52] The face of Christianity is changing, but it appears to be in good hands. The Muslim church is reaping much of the rewards of the rapid growth of the African population, but Jenkins argues that in terms of reproduction rates in Africa, the Christian church is outpacing the Islamic people.[53] *Publishers Weekly* reports, "In a meticulously researched study, Jenkins examines the reasons that Christian churches are booming in these countries. One of the main reasons, he argues, is that Christianity in these developing nations focuses less on doctrine and church politics and more on the ways that religion weaves itself into daily life."[54]

HOPE FOR THE FUTURE

Some discouraging numbers and thoughts have been documented in this chapter because the church needs a reality check. Only then will it begin to understand the pit it is in and find a way to get out of it, but the church is not in danger of death. It is built on the solid rock of Jesus Christ, and "the gates of Hades will not conquer it" (Matt 16:18). Paul writes, "His intent was that now, through the church, the manifold wisdom of God should be made known to the rulers and authorities in the heavenly realms, according to his eternal purpose that he accomplished in Christ Jesus our Lord" (Eph 3:10–11). The church will succeed, not only to spread the gospel in this world but to glorify God beyond this world. The church isn't an iteration of God's plan—it is his plan. The church is the bride of Christ. We are the bride of Christ, not individually but together; not our denomination of the church but the whole; not those who are living exactly like the bride should live but all of God's children.

The church is in desperate need of a new generation of optimistic leaders who will change the landscape of Christian ministry in America. This book will provide a potential method of course correction, beginning with a shift in perspective by way of theological and attitude correction. Speculative eschatological views that lead Christians to disdain the world they live

---

52. Jenkins, *Next Christendom*, 2.

53. Jenkins, *Next Christendom*, 9.

54. "Next Christendom," para. 1.

in, pessimism about the future of the Christian church, and cynicism about the potential adoption of pre-Christians have had an unintended, negative impact on the church's ability to fulfill its Great Commission.

The next chapter will discuss the effects pessimism and cynicism have had on church growth. The coach of a sports team may fear his team is going to lose a game, but it would be counterproductive to communicate that fear to his team unless he is certain the loss is inevitable. Otherwise, the news itself is likely to cause the feared, negative outcome. Jesus will return, and although humans don't know what his return will look like, "it won't be just to extract cowering saints from the rubble of a forsaken planet, [and] it won't be to evacuate a bunch of me-focused consumers so [they] can live on a cloud."[55] To see Paul's description of Christians going to the clouds to welcome their king back to earth as a description of an evacuation is, at best, simply an assumption (1 Thess 4:16–17).

DISCUSSION QUESTIONS:

a. What are your thoughts about the current state of the church in America? Is it declining?

b. Do you think Christians are negative people or is that a misperception non-Christians have of us?

c. How can Christians be full of grace and truth in the homosexual conversation?

d. What can the church do to change the way outsiders think of us? Is that even a worthwhile endeavor?

55. McNall, *Long Story Short*, 165.

4

Negativity Leads to Cynicism and Division

Better to be wrong about something big than right about trivialities . . . Every person who has revolutionized history has not spent their time arguing over trivialities, but dared to declare big dreams and decrees. And every one (Augustine, Aquinas, Luther, Calvin, Wesley, etc.) was wrong about something big.[1]

—LEONARD SWEET

CYNICISM IS UNAPPEALING

PESSIMISM IS NOT THE only antonym of optimism listed in Webster's dictionary. Cynicism is there too. Cynicism is interpersonal pessimism. Pessimism is usually pointed at circumstances. Cynicism is pointed at people. In other words, cynicism is judgmental pessimism.

In the first part of Philippians 4, the apostle Paul turns his attention to the importance of relationships to positivity as he tells the church that his joy comes from his relationship with them.

> Therefore, my dear brothers and sisters, stay true to the Lord. I
> love you and long to see you, dear friends, for you are my joy and

1. Sweet, "Better to Be Wrong."

the crown I receive for my work. Now I appeal to Euodia and Syntyche. Please, because you belong to the Lord, settle your disagreement. And I ask you, my true partner, to help these two women, for they worked hard with me in telling others the Good News. They worked along with Clement and the rest of my coworkers, whose names are written in the Book of Life. Always be full of joy in the Lord. I say it again—rejoice! Let everyone see that you are considerate in all you do. Remember, the Lord is coming soon. Don't worry about anything; instead, pray about everything. Tell God what you need, and thank him for all he has done. Then you will experience God's peace, which exceeds anything we can understand. His peace will guard your hearts and minds as you live in Christ Jesus. And now, dear brothers and sisters, one final thing. Fix your thoughts on what is true, and honorable, and right, and pure, and lovely, and admirable. Think about things that are excellent and worthy of praise. (Phil 4:1–8 NLT)

Euodia and Syntyche were two Christian women in Philippi who had a disagreement. In this passage, the apostle Paul is asking them to get past their disagreement. Paul teaches that disunity in the church will undermine the mission of the church. He didn't take a side in the argument; he focused on unity. Paul's famous exhortation to think about things that are excellent and worthy of praise is a statement about unity. He is telling them that by focusing on their disagreement, they are damaging the church and their witness, and verse 7 reveals the peace that goes beyond understanding comes when we are considerate of others, put aside worry, ask God to provide for our needs, and focus our minds on things that are good.

When people predict that the decline of the church is inevitable, they are forced to come up with excuses when the church grows. When that happens, we repel pre-Christians. A Baptist pastor who was apparently eager to divide the body of Christ once told me Christians who don't believe in a literal, seven-day creation are not actually Christians. The most common divisions in the church are over secondary theologies such as election, spiritual gifts, revelation, and church governance, and infighting about ideas like these is terribly unattractive to pre-Christians. Who would want to be adopted into a family that fights all the time? I regularly get emails from people who say our church shouldn't play songs by Bethel or Hillsong because their theology is wrong. If we can only sing songs by people whose theology matches ours, that will be the end of music in the church. Those who attempt to draw the line between wrong theology and theology that is so wrong it should be boycotted have slipped into an unhealthy level of theological arrogance.

When Christians become convinced the church will face opposition that will lead to the decline of Christianity, they become cynical and skeptical of churches that grow. If it is believed Christianity will continue to grow, it is logical that churches will get larger. In that case, it is reassuring that the world is experiencing an incredible increase in large churches. When people believe Christianity will soon begin to decline, they search for corruption in growing churches, because the growth of large churches does not align with their pessimism.

Cynicism shouldn't be allowed to repel pre-Christians, and it must not be allowed to keep Christians from optimistic partnership with people who share core beliefs. Leonard Sweet writes,

> Because I suspect some of our 22nd century kids may live to be 170, I looked at what the church was talking about 170 years ago. In my tribe (Methodist), one of the biggest issues consuming local churches in 1847 was "promiscuous seating" at church, by which they meant the radical notion that families (including children) could sit together in worship, not just separate seating for women and children on one side of the church, and men on the other. In 1847 it was causing splits in churches and charges of heresy, tearing apart communities, causing civil war in families, and wasn't "resolved" until the 1852 general conference. So I wonder . . . how many of our holy hullabaloos today will look just as ridiculous 100 or 150 or 170 years from now as this holy hullabaloo back then?[2]

If Christians are distracted, fighting among themselves, how will they learn to set an example of hospitality and progress to the rest of the world? New Testament history "is full of fruitful dialogue and debate between sisters and brothers of good faith who wrestled with each other's views and profited from the open dialogue in the end."[3]

The Christian Temple

Perhaps the best description of biblical unity is found in 1 Corinthians 3. It begins with a rebuke of Christians who divided themselves rather than serving God as a united body:

2. Sweet, "Because I Suspect."

3. DeSilva, *Introduction to the New Testament*, 463.

> Brothers and sisters, I could not address you as people who live
> by the Spirit but as people who are still worldly—mere infants in
> Christ. I gave you milk, not solid food, for you were not yet ready
> for it. Indeed, you are still not ready. You are still worldly. For since
> there is jealousy and quarreling among you, are you not worldly?
> Are you not acting like mere humans? (1 Cor 3:13)

Spiritual immaturity is described as jealousy. Christians who quarrel
are described as worldly. Paul continues:

> For when one says, "I follow Paul," and another, "I follow Apol-
> los," are you not mere human beings? What, after all, is Apollos?
> And what is Paul? Only servants, through whom you came to be-
> lieve—as the Lord has assigned to each his task. I planted the seed,
> Apollos watered it, but God has been making it grow. So neither
> the one who plants nor the one who waters is anything, but only
> God, who makes things grow. The one who plants and the one
> who waters have one purpose, and they will each be rewarded ac-
> cording to their own labor. For we are coworkers in God's service;
> you are God's field, God's building. By the grace God has given me,
> I laid a foundation as a wise builder, and someone else is building
> on it. But each one should build with care. For no one can lay any
> foundation other than the one already laid, which is Jesus Christ.
> (1 Cor 3:4–11)

We are coworkers in God's service. We are on the same team. Why
are we so tempted to divide the body of Christ by choosing to follow men?
John Calvin and John Wesley were great leaders, but they were servants of
Christ. Division based on opinions of their teachings reveals spiritual immaturity. The same is true about Andy Stanley, John Piper, Douglas Wilson,
and Rick Warren. Paul continues:

> If anyone builds on this foundation using gold, silver, costly stones,
> wood, hay or straw, their work will be shown for what it is, because
> the Day will bring it to light. It will be revealed with fire, and the
> fire will test the quality of each person's work. If what has been
> built survives, the builder will receive a reward. If it is burned up,
> the builder will suffer loss but yet will be saved—even though only
> as one escaping through the flames. (1 Cor 3:12–15)

There are occasions where the persistent teaching of a gospel that is
contrary to the gospel taught by Jesus Christ must be rejected. This has
happened regularly in the history of Christianity, with good results. In
Galatians 1:9, Paul abandons his regular hospitable approach to say, "As

we have already said, so now I say again: If anybody is preaching to you a gospel other than what you accepted, let them be under God's curse!" The curse is God's curse, not ours, and Paul is referring to the primary Christian belief, not a secondary theology.

I do believe multiple secondary Christian theologies are harmful to the Christian mission, including the prosperity gospel, legalism, and dispensationalism. You could easily add to this list. With that said, I have many friends who preach those theologies. I have been in aggressive conversations with some of them, and I did my best to convince them of their error. Those arguments may be beneficial, but a person is almost never convinced to change his or her opinion because of an argument. Even when we disagree with our Christian brothers and sisters, it is God's job to judge them, not ours. Too many Christians have erred on the side of division and judgment rather than hospitality and dialogue in order to win internal squabbles that serve no other purpose but to bolster personal pride. The divisions that have resulted from these disagreements have fractured the church into many denominations that people are forced to choose between in order to join the Christian church in America.

In 1 Corinthians 3:16, Paul describes the church as something that cannot be divided without breaking it, a temple:

> Don't you know that you yourselves are God's temple and that God's Spirit dwells in your midst? If anyone destroys God's temple, God will destroy that person; for God's temple is sacred, and you together are that temple. Do not deceive yourselves. If any of you think you are wise by the standards of this age, you should become "fools" so that you may become wise. For the wisdom of this world is foolishness in God's sight. As it is written: "He catches the wise in their craftiness"; and again, "The Lord knows that the thoughts of the wise are futile." So then, no more boasting about human leaders! All things are yours, whether Paul or Apollos or Cephas or the world or life or death or the present or the future—all are yours, and you are of Christ, and Christ is of God. (1 Cor 3:16–23)

Division based on the teachings of men and secondary Christian theologies has become a common habit of the church, and this under the guise of creating a more perfect union. When we break the body of Christ, we nail Christ to the cross.

Rampant Division

There are hundreds of Christian denominations in the United States alone. This is a problem because that many divisions will repel pre-Christians. In *The Paradox of Choice*, Barry Schwartz makes the case that having too many options actually causes people to avoid making a choice.[4] People who go to purchase something but are faced with too many options avoid purchasing. This problem is compounded when the people offering the various choices claim there is something wrong with the other options being offered.[5] The Christian church in America is at a minimum failing to keep up with population growth. Could that be, in part, because pre-Christians assume the many options (or versions) of Christianity imply there is no singular truth, despite what most of them claim? Could it also be Christian leaders have become most passionate about ideas and secondary theologies most people don't care about?

A majority of church leaders would agree there are too many denominations in Christianity, but they continue to hold tight to the secondary theologies that caused many of the denominational divides in the first place. The topics of the arguments are tedious but Christians stick to their guns while claiming they are protecting their parishioners from a slippery slope that could lead their followers to heresy. When did it become the church's job to be the arbiter and keeper of all facts? When did it become the church's job to tell people what conclusions they can and cannot come to in their search for truth? When the church insisted on controlling all truth, the Reformation was necessary. The Christian mandate is to make disciples, but the desire to have huddles of people bunkered together who all have the exact same beliefs has hindered the church's ability to reach people who would otherwise become those disciples. Jennie Harrop writes, "Jesus came in part to clarify that the us versus them dichotomy we so easily slide into is not only erroneous but dangerous; two millennia later, the challenge has intensified."[6] Ed Stetzer writes, "Secondary issues have conflated the spiritual and the natural in a way that weakens our witness and embroils us in deep conflict that distracts from and distorts the gospel of Jesus. Unflinching devotion to a tribe not only pushes us to fight against

---

4. Schwartz, *Paradox of Choice*, 3.

5. DeSilva, *Introduction to the New Testament*, 463.

6. Harrop, *Jesus Quotient*, 430.

issues that are not connected to the gospel and don't advance the mission of God, but it also affects how we view others who disagree with us."[7]

In my experience, people who have chosen sides on the largest number of minute theologies neglect ministry to pre-Christians. Perhaps it's time to choose fewer battles and focus on the mandate, and if it's politics, bureaucracy, and money that keep sects from uniting, then priorities must change.

I am writing this paragraph in the middle of the COVID-19 pandemic, and Marty's church has just called me to tell me he is reopening his church building this Sunday. Marty is the pastor of a great church not too far from our church, and he's one of the awesome people who helped me through a nervous breakdown after I became the lead pastor of New Life. Meanwhile, I am currently sitting on my couch with a high fever, wondering if I have COVID-19. Like many pastors, I'm worried about two things: I'm worried Marty's church is going to open before our church and take all our people, but I'm also worried if we open our church a lot of people will get sick. (I know pastors aren't supposed to worry, but we do.) So here's my confession: when worry creeps in, it's tempting to adopt militant rhetoric. I want to say, "Churches that open too soon are putting their congregations in danger, and if you go to those churches, you are complicit." In my warped mind, that would scare some of my people out of leaving to go to Marty's church, and it may even scare a few of his people into coming to my church. But I won't say that, or anything like it. In fact, I will publicly praise him for his bravery and faith because I know his church can reach people that mine can't. Go get 'em Marty.

HOSPITALITY

Infighting in the church has caused Christians to lose sight of what the world has long known about the importance of hospitality to success. What is it about Christians that makes pre-Christians think so negatively about them? One contributing factor is the hostility they believe Christians have toward their ideas. In *God Space*, Doug Pollock writes, "Essentially, we are sending the culture this message: Not only do we not endorse your point of view, we also don't accept you. This lack of acceptance crushes opportunities for spiritual conversations."[8] Jesus Christ was able to walk with sinners

7. Stetzer, *Christians in the Age of Outrage*, 15.

8. Pollock, *God Space*, 31.

without repelling them with judgmentalism. Instead, while making his high standards clear, he showed them extravagant hospitality and grace that led them to repentance.

The alternative to the common habit of prideful hardheadedness is persistent hospitality and grace that agrees to disagree and works together without full agreement. Jesus, knowing Judas would betray him, washed Judas's feet and said, "Now that I, your Lord and Teacher, have washed your feet, you also should wash one another's feet" (John 13:14). Hospitality was of prime importance to the early Christians. The church was even spoken of as "God's household" (1 Tim 3:15). It is not surprising, then, that early Christians welcomed "traveling Christians, itinerant preachers, and other strangers into the church."[9] Hospitality was not only a method for welcoming diverse ideas, it was also the means through which they exercised charitable activity within the fellowship of the local church and within the larger context of their community.

The church should not blame pre-Christians for their view of the church. Their views are influenced by the hypocrisy and judgmentalism of the church, but they are also influenced by their fallen nature. It should be no surprise that pre-Christians are resistant to the gospel message (2 Tim 3:2). We don't blame a lion for killing a zebra, and we don't blame babies for crying in church (though we have discovered strategies to counteract the distractions of babies crying in church). Dr. Thomas Sowell says, we don't blame "plane crashes on gravity. Certainly, planes wouldn't crash if it wasn't for gravity. But when thousands of planes fly millions of miles every day without crashing, explaining why a particular plane crashed because of gravity gets you nowhere."[10] Gravity is a constant. The resistance of pre-Christians to Christ is a constant, but that does not mean the church owns none of the blame for their resistance. The church also cannot blame its lack of growth on the resistance or sinfulness of pre-Christians unless it believes the Holy Spirit has stopped preparing hearts for the gospel message. The effective church counters resistance with grace, truth, and hospitality.

Christians have not been given the mandate to judge who is saved, who is chosen, or who is justified. We have been given the joyful directive to offer Christlike hospitality to the whole world.

9. Martin and Davids, *Dictionary of the Later New Testament*, 504.

10. Sowell, "Random Thoughts," para. 4..

Come as You are

Rather than condemn them for their sinful behavior, Jesus ate with sinners, while the Pharisees separated themselves from them and criticized them (Mark 2). Instead of teaching them not to drink too much alcohol, Jesus provided more wine to the people at the wedding in Cana (John 2). Rather than condemn them for worshiping an idol to an "unknown god," Paul met the religious leaders on common ground when he told them on Mars Hill about the almighty God (Acts 17). To be in relationship with Jesus is to be in relationship with the world.

Romans 12:13–21 says,

> Share with the Lord's people who are in need. Practice hospitality. Bless those who persecute you; bless and do not curse. Rejoice with those who rejoice; mourn with those who mourn. Live in harmony with one another. Do not be proud, but be willing to associate with people of low position. Do not be conceited. Do not repay anyone evil for evil. Be careful to do what is right in the eyes of everyone. If it is possible, as far as it depends on you, live at peace with everyone. Do not take revenge, my dear friends, but leave room for God's wrath, for it is written: "It is mine to avenge; I will repay," says the Lord. On the contrary: "If your enemy is hungry, feed him; if he is thirsty, give him something to drink. In doing this, you will heap burning coals on his head." Do not be overcome by evil, but overcome evil with good.

The human conflict is that although in our core we are the same, on the surface we create barriers and conditions for sharing and receiving love. According to Jesus' example, we are called to welcome all people and challenge ourselves to love one another because we are more alike than we are different. In his letter to the Philippians, Paul writes,

> Don't be selfish; don't try to impress others. Be humble, thinking of others as better than yourselves. Don't look out only for your own interests, but take an interest in others, too. You must have the same attitude that Christ Jesus had. Though he was God, he did not think of equality with God as something to cling to. Instead, he gave up his divine privileges; he took the humble position of a slave and was born as a human being. When he appeared in human form, he humbled himself in obedience to God and died a criminal's death on a cross (Phil 2:3–8).

The churches in America that have truly adopted a mission that invites people to "come as you are" or "belong before you believe" have seen numerical growth.[11] Rather than confronting people with cynicism, these churches allow people to bring their ideas with them to church. Andy Stanley says the church is in the environment-creating business, building on-ramps for people to begin their journey with Jesus Christ.[12] "While those of us in the church may believe we offer good on-ramps for everyone, this is not the word on the street."[13] It will take a change in approach to change the perception that the church is full of cynical, judgmental people, because our previous actions have at least indirectly contributed to these perceptions.

What were those previous actions? In boycotting, protesting, and demonizing everything they didn't like, Christians looked like negative, angry people. They forgot the joy that should come with salvation and instead prioritized chastity, poverty, separateness, and self-righteousness (disguised as holiness), and, perhaps the most harmful of all, overspiritualized sacred traditions. The gospel is good news, but the Christian church made it look like bad news.

It's time for Christians to stop boycotting. Christians built idols to "cancel culture" long before Twitter made it mainstream. We just called it boycotting. When I was young we couldn't shop at Kmart or Target because of a few items they sold in their stores. We routinely stood on street corners shouting about how much God hates abortion. Not too long ago Christians were encouraged to boycott the Muppets because of a joke they told, Starbucks because they used a red cup, and PetSmart because they didn't say Merry Christmas. This list goes on and on. The goal of Christianity isn't to completely separate from a sinful world—the goal is to shape that world.

Eschatology

After years of deciding what I believe on many different theologies, the last area of theology that I brought myself to study is eschatology. That's because it's incredibly complex and impossibly vague, and I often think it's a topic God doesn't want us to pick a side on. Eschatology is the study of educated guessing about the events that will happen before, during, and after the second coming of Jesus Christ. That's my definition. I managed to graduate

11. Burke, *No Perfect People Allowed*, 20.

12. Stanley, *Deep & Wide*, 203.

13. Pollock, *God Space*, 12.

with two theology degrees before I took an interest in eschatology. Before I started studying it for myself, I just accepted what I read in the *Left Behind* books. That's what everyone else around me believed, so I assumed it was biblical truth. The problem came when I actually started studying it. I could not find what I read in the *Left Behind* books in the Bible, and after studying the various theories about what's going to happen when Jesus returns, I just decided I really don't think any of them are completely correct. It may frustrate you to hear that I'm not going to argue for any one eschatological theory in this book. My goal is actually to argue that Christians should not put their faith in any of the interpretations of end-times prophecies. God told Job the universe is too complex for us to comprehend its beauty, and I believe God's plan for our future is even more complex than the world we see.

Before Jesus came to Earth, the Jews memorized the Hebrew Scriptures, trying to figure out what it was trying to tell them. The Hebrew Scriptures are packed full of predictions about a Messiah that would come and save the Hebrew people. They spent their lives trying to predict who the Messiah was going to be and when he would come, but even with all their interpreting and predicting they still missed him. Prophesies are often incredibly confusing, and we usually can't understand them until the prophesied event happens. Hindsight is usually the best interpreter. Maybe we are simply meant to live with excitement about Christ's return, and work every day in anticipation.

DISCUSSION QUESTIONS:

a. How do you feel about the fact there are so many Christian denominations and theological divisions? Do you believe these divisions are harmful or helpful?

b. What issues/theologies, if any, are worth dividing churches over?

c. Can a church be effective if its members do not agree on multiple theologies?

d. How do you think disunity inside the church affects the church's ability to accomplish its mission?

5

Dispensationalism

Regardless of one's position with respect to a cultural mandate, historically some evangelicals have tended to focus so much on an attempt to pin down the precise timing of Christ's *parousia* [second coming] that they have failed to engage in the kind of gospel demonstration (i.e., social action) necessary for many lost and hurting people in our world to be able to really "hear" the good news of God's love being proclaimed to them.[1]

—GARY TYRA

THERE WERE FIVE SECONDS left on the clock, and my high school basketball team was down by one point. The other team was at the free throw line shooting a one-and-one. Our team needed them to miss a free throw. Then we needed a rebound and a made shot. Sure enough, they missed the free throw, my twin brother grabbed the rebound, threw the ball across the court to me, and I drained a shot just before the buzzer sounded! The crowd erupted with excitement, but we lost the game. Why? Because I hit the last-second shot before the halftime buzzer. When endings approach, timing becomes more important, and that will be the last time I relive my high school glory days in this book.

---

1. Tyra, *Missional Orthodoxy*, 331.

Eschatology is the study of the future of the world and the destiny of humanity; therefore, conversations about pessimism and optimism depend largely on eschatological predictions. There is a lot of disagreement in the church about what will happen before, during, and after the second coming of Jesus Christ. This book will not select and defend a single eschatological theory, but a conversation about the role pessimistic eschatology has played in contributing to the church's image problem is warranted, because the pessimism that chilling predictions of future terror produces leads conservative evangelicals in America to militant bunkering rather than energized evangelizing.

The future isn't usually as bad as our fears tell us it will be, and the past is not usually as good as we remember it being. Conversations about the good ol' days are almost always riddled with false memories, and conspiracy theories about the future are almost always overstated. Jennie Harrop writes, "Doomsayers rarely bring anything productive to a conversation, and yet Christians have consistently stood at the forefront, decrying the culture and pining for the better years of yesterday."[2] We must not allow our inability to remember reality and our fear about the future to determine how we interpret biblical prophecies.

For that reason, the church's eschatological communication should reflect the discernment of John in Revelation 10. In a world tempted to publicly share every thought on social media, it seems absurd to believe someone could keep a revelation from God secret, but John of Patmos did just that when he said, "And when the seven thunders spoke, I was about to write; but I heard a voice from heaven say, 'Seal up what the seven thunders have said and do not write it down'" (Rev 10:4). In this world, we won't know the contents of that revelation, but the censoring itself teaches the church a beneficial lesson: it's unlikely the message of the seven thunders revealed the accuracy of left behind theology, and it is possible the disclosure of the thunders' message would have caused more confusion than clarity. About this censoring Joshua McNall writes, "The command seems somewhat odd, since John is elsewhere ordered to 'write' what he had seen, regardless of its strange or controversial content. Yet in this one instance, just as he is about to click the button labeled 'Publish,' the voice of God chimes in—'Don't do it!'"[3]

---

2. Harrop, *Jesus Quotient*, 550.

3. McNall, "What Seven Thunders Spoke," para. 4.

The proponents of theologies that lead to belief in an inevitable decline in Christian discipleship, conspiracy theories of an antichrist around every corner, and the futility of graceful correction are given the option to practice similar restraint. One eschatology that should only be shared with extreme caution is premillennial dispensationalism. Dispensationalism is an eschatological theory developed by harmonizing Revelation 20:16, 1 Thessalonians 4:15–17, and other passages. It is the left behind theology, the version of premillennialism that includes a seven-year period of tribulation between the rapture and second coming of Jesus. It is possible dispensationalism is an accurate interpretation of biblical prophecy, but because we can't be sure and because dispensationalism has a tendency to lead people to negativity, restraint in teaching the belief as absolute fact is necessary.

Eschatology Theories

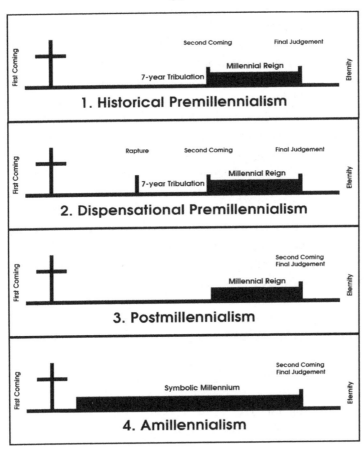

65

ESCHATOLOGY AND MISSIOLOGY

In *A Missional Orthodoxy*, Gary Tyra points out there is a "crucial connection" between eschatology and missiology.[4] Eschatology is theology concerned with how and when the final judgment of souls will happen. A Christian's eschatology affects his or her mission effectiveness, and the tone and topic of the vision-casting of many Christians has kept young people, prodigals, and skeptics from listening to the Christian message. In a culture where it is not in vogue to be the favored team, prideful confidence in a belief is a repellent to many people, especially the younger generations.[5] Still, the majority of Christians in America have confidently espoused a single, unsubstantiated conclusion that is leading the church to an undesirable fate.[6] That eschatological theory has been labeled dispensationalism, or left behind theology.

On a topic as challenging and diverse as eschatology, a wise theologian would admit his probability of being at least partially wrong, yet many have clung to dispensationalism as absolute truth. Christians who prioritize the Great Commission will avoid arrogant defense of a specific eschatological theory. Although his eschatological conclusions come too close to universalism, Brian McLaren points out that dispensational eschatology (or what he calls the "eschatology of abandonment") "marginalize[s] Jesus with all his talk of the kingdom of God coming to earth, being among us, and being acceptable today," and a more optimistic eschatology will lead to "an engaging gospel of the kingdom" and a recognition that "people matter."[7]

In a lecture about eschatology, Dr. John Drury said, "Our beliefs about the future determine our perspective on the present."[8] Pessimistic eschatology can cause the church to assume mission failure is inevitable and miss out on the benefits of positivity. The authors of the New Testament books never said the birth of Jesus introduced a steady decline of humanity that would end in the second coming of Jesus Christ, but the authors of the entirety of the Christian Scriptures introduce a long narrative of history that culminates in the physical reunification of God and his children. If the church is able to leave the door open to optimistic interpretations of

---

4. Tyra, *Missional Orthodoxy*, 333.

5. Kinnaman and Lyons, *Unchristian*, 19.

6. Barrick, "Poll," para. 2.

7. McLaren, *Generous Orthodoxy*, 236238.

8. Drury, "Lecture 8.1."

eschatological prophecies, it will be more likely to take advantage of the benefits of positivity.

Christ's optimistic messaging made Christianity "the single greatest movement in the history of the world,"[9] and the idea made popular by the *Left Behind* books, that this movement will be ended when Jesus Christ returns to "rapture" a relatively small group of people before a tribulation, is a "recent novelty in church history."[10] In fact, "the Bible knows nothing of a preliminary return of Christ prior to his final return."[11] Nevertheless, rapture theology has become "widespread in evangelical churches" with little backing in Christian Scripture.[12] The antagonistic tone of the church, seen most evidently in dispensational theologies, has shaken the church on its foundation. Is it any surprise the judgmental people of Westboro Baptist Church are dispensationalists, and many Christian leaders who espoused more optimistic eschatological beliefs helped Christianity to become such a great movement (see chapter 9)?[13]

Although dispensationalism is "on the wane" in academic circles, a majority of Christians seem to be content with the comfort that results from the belief that Christians will not be around to suffer the wrath of the antichrist or the punishment awaiting those who do not live the life Christians are prone to believe they must live.[14] The rise of dispensationalism in America came from pessimistic thinking that resulted from the horrors of the Spanish Flu, World War I, the Great Depression, World War II, the Cold War, and war in the Middle East,[15] and it is stories of persecution and pain that are causing dispensationalism to spread so rapidly across the Global South. The Pew Research Center found 58 percent of white evangelical Christians say Jesus Christ will definitely or probably return to earth before 2050, and 41 percent of all Americans believe Jesus Christ will definitely or probably return to earth before 2050.[16] Even if these people do not know their predictions of future events affect their outlook on life, it must. If a

---

9. Craig, "#439 Christian Pessimism?," para. 4.

10. Craig, "#439 Christian Pessimism?," para. 5.

11. Craig, "#439 Christian Pessimism?," para. 5.

12. Craig, "#439 Christian Pessimism?," para. 5.

13. Ayoub, "Harold Camping," para. 5.

14. Riddlebarger, *Case for Amillennialism*, 27.

15. Riddlebarger, *Case for Amillennialism*, 26.

16. Pew Research Center, "Jesus Christ's Return to Earth," para. 1.

parent does not believe his or her children will be on this earth for long, there is less incentive to work to make the world a better place for them.

Involuntary Responses

I faint. When I see blood, when I get a shot, when I'm watching TV shows with surgeries, when I take a CPR class, when I twist my ankle, when old women describe their surgeries, and when Leonardo DiCaprio gets mauled by a bear, I faint (all true stories). It's an involuntary response. I asked my doctor what causes me to faint when I see a wound. She said it's a subconscious response. When I see a wound, my subconscious tells my heart I am bleeding, and my heart slows down so I don't bleed out. I'm sure it's much more complicated than that, but that is how she simplified the concept for me to understand.

Advocates of pessimistic theologies are often unaware of how their belief that decline is inevitable or that Christians will soon abandon Earth affects their behavior. As humans work toward goals, our subconscious judges the achievability of those goals. When our subconscious determines the goal is achievable, our involuntary response is to give more brain power, energy, and determination to achieve that goal. "The closer you perceive a target to be . . . the faster you move toward it."[17] When our subconscious allows the full extent of our emotional and intellectual power to be unleashed to solve a problem or attack a goal, our likelihood of success greatly increases.

LEFT BEHIND

Because the *Left Behind* books were written to illustrate the complicated version of eschatology known as dispensationalism, the first book ended with an obvious cliffhanger and multiple other books were planned. The series concluded after the sixteenth bestselling book was released and sold close to 80 million books.[18] To those who were familiar with the books when they were being released, it may seem the influence of the series has waned, but their influence in the Global South is actually increasing. The influence of the books also increases when its readers grow in influence

17. Achor, *Before Happiness*, 109.

18. Domonoske, "Tim LaHaye," para. 7.

because the *Left Behind* books have been treated by many people as theology books.

In 2000, Cloud Ten Pictures made the first book into a movie, and the influence of the series increased. Although the reviews of the movie were negative, the movie earned $4.2 million at the box office, and the success led to the production of two sequels, a video game, and in 2014 a remake starring Nicolas Cage. The books were obviously works of fiction, but because the authors attempted to reflect their personal predictions in the writings, many faithful readers chose to trust the intellect and biblical understanding of the authors. The story itself is very scary but has a hopeful ending for the heroes of the story, the Christians. The ending is not hopeful for people who are not Christians and for people who are empathetic enough to dread the pain, death, and eternal torture of millions of unbelievers.

The books portray a world that is "spiraling downward in a satanic free fall."[19] That is dangerous because if Christians don't believe they can stop that free fall, they may resist engagement with culture. If the world will soon be ruled by the antichrist, it will tempt Christians to become separatists, "establishing their own subcultures, rather than trying to influence the culture in which they find themselves . . . Their temptation . . . will be to ignore their callings to be salt and light in the secular arena."[20]

The genre of the books is a mix of thriller and science fiction that causes tremendous fear for the reader. The story begins in Israel in a modern-day fictional world that is experiencing widespread famine, war, and sinfulness, and that turmoil is causing people to consider the possibility of a one-world government. While Buck Williams, a journalist, is interviewing a scientist who has discovered a way to make any soil on Earth easy to farm, a war breaks out in Israel and a mysterious old man warns Buck that the war is the beginning of a seven-year Armageddon. The reader is then introduced to Rayford Steele, a married pilot whose is having an affair with an attractive flight attendant. On a flight to London, Steele witnesses the strange disappearance of some of the passengers on his jet. On the ground below, chaos breaks out as people all over the world disappear, including people who were driving cars, flying airplanes, directing airplanes, and doing other dangerous things. Steele's Christian wife and children also disappear. The reader is then introduced to Nicolae Carpathia, a political leader

19. Veith, "When Truth Gets Left Behind," para. 24.
20. Veith, "When Truth Gets Left Behind," para. 24.

from the United Nations who has promised to restore peace and stability to the world.

The rest of the series follows the adventures of the Tribulation Force, made up of postrapture converted Christians including Buck Williams, Rayford Steele, and a pastor who was not worthy to be raptured with the other Christians. The Tribulation Force attempts to resist the antichrist and lead the world to faith in Jesus. Over the course of sixteen books, the reader experiences a fictional version of what LaHaye and Jenkins believe will happen in the future. Those events include a seven-year tribulation, another second coming of Jesus, a millennium of God reigning on Earth, and a final judgment of all people. The action becomes increasingly intense with each book. For a while, believers are spared, but when Nicolae Carpathia is killed and rises from the dead, even the Christians are subjected to suffering.

The tremendous popularity of the books caused millions of Christians, including me, to treat the books as a guide to understanding what Scripture says about the future of the world. The problem is a large majority of theologians do not agree with LaHaye's interpretation of Scripture. In fact, only one-third of pastors believe the theology of the *Left Behind* books is accurate.[21]

When my dad was a young adult, having grown up in a church that heavily taught dispensationalism, he had regular dreams about the rapture. In his dreams, he would begin to float toward heaven, but he would hit the ceiling and fall back to his bed. He and his friends were confident they were doomed to hell, or at the very least doomed to have their heads cut off by the antichrist. Throughout my life, I have heard him tell stories of the terror dispensationalism caused. My mom, who might be the most innocent person I've ever known, experienced the same fear. Even though I am a Christian, the belief that Jesus will secretly rapture all dedicated Christians and all children, leaving behind the false Christians and unbeliever to wrecked cars and childless mothers, is terrifying, but the fact that it is terrifying does not necessarily make it wrong. The next chapter will be an examination of its viability.

21. Smietana, "Only One-Third," para. 3.

Pessimism about the Future of the Church

ANSWER CHOICES	RESPONSES ▼	
▼ Hostility toward Christianity in the world is increasing.	81.36%	48
▼ Sinfulness in the world is increasing.	69.49%	41
▼ Violence in the world is increasing.	62.71%	37
▼ Hostility toward Christianity will continue to increase until Jesus returns.	69.49%	41
▼ Sinfulness will continue to increase until Jesus returns.	64.41%	38
▼ Violence will continue to increase until Jesus returns.	54.24%	32
▼ Hostility toward Christianity in the world is decreasing.	8.47%	5
▼ Sinfulness in the world is decreasing.	3.39%	2
▼ Violence in the world is decreasing.	11.86%	7
▼ Hostility toward Christianity will continue to decrease until Jesus returns.	1.69%	1
▼ Sinfulness will continue to decrease until Jesus returns.	1.69%	1
▼ Violence will continue to decrease until Jesus returns.	3.39%	2

Total Respondents: 59

In 2018, I performed an anonymous survey on Facebook of fifty-nine of my colleagues (pastors in The Wesleyan Church).[22] The primary purpose of the survey was to ask them what they think about hostility toward Christianity, sinfulness, and violence in the world. Forty-eight of them (81.4 percent) think "hostility toward Christianity in the world is increasing," while only 8.5 percent believe "hostility toward Christianity in the world is decreasing." Forty-one (69.5 percent) think "hostility toward Christianity will continue to increase until Jesus returns," and only one (1.7 percent) thinks "hostility toward Christianity will continue to decrease until Jesus returns."

Forty-one (69.5 percent) think sinfulness in the world is increasing, and only two (3.4 percent) think sinfulness in the world is decreasing. Thirty-eight (64.4 percent) think "sinfulness will continue to increase until Jesus returns," and only one (1.7 percent) thinks "sinfulness will continue to decrease until Jesus returns."

The most revealing result shows they are out of touch with reality. Thirty-seven (62.7 percent) think "violence in the world is increasing," while only seven (11.9 percent) think "violence in the world is decreasing." Thirty-two (54.2 percent) think "violence in the world will continue to increase until Jesus returns," and only two (3.4 percent) that "violence will

22. See Appendix A.

continue to decrease until Jesus returns." Violence in the world is obviously decreasing.

Sin Decreasing

Historically speaking, it is difficult to make the case that our world is not becoming more peaceful. Jim Geraghty, in an article titled "There are a Lot of Reasons to Feel Optimistic about America's Future," writes, "We fear terrorism, but one of the reasons that terrorism and asymmetrical warfare are rising is because conventional war is growing rarer."[23]

On the topic of violence and war, Steven Pinker explains that

> Tribal warfare was nine times as deadly as war and genocide in the 20th century. The murder rate in medieval Europe was more than thirty times what it is today. Slavery, sadistic punishments, and frivolous executions were unexceptionable features of life for millennia, then were suddenly abolished. Wars between developed countries have vanished, and even in the developing world, wars kill a fraction of the numbers they did a few decades ago. Rape, hate crimes, deadly riots, child abuse—all substantially down.[24]

Human nature leads people to fear the worst outcome and think pessimistically about the potential for positive outcomes, but HumanProgress. org reports

> Evidence from individual scholars, academic institutions, and international organizations shows dramatic improvements in human well-being throughout much of the world. In recent decades, these improvements have been especially striking in developing countries. Unfortunately, there is often a wide gap between the reality of human experience, which is characterized by incremental improvements, and public perception, which tends to be quite negative about the current state of the world and skeptical about humanity's future prospects.[25]

Brian Wang reports the results of the research of Laurence Chandy and Geoffrey Gertz, which says

---

23. Geraghty, "There are a Lot of Reasons," para. 9.

24. Pinker, *Better Angels of Our Nature*, para. 1.

25. "What We Do," para. 2.

[The] rise of emerging economies has led to a dramatic fall in global poverty . . . [The authors] estimate that between 2005 and 2010, the total number of poor people around the world fell by nearly half a billion, from over 1.3 billion in 2005 to under 900 million in 2010. Poverty reduction of this magnitude is unparalleled in history: never before have so many people been lifted out of poverty over such a brief period of time.[26]

As long as extreme poverty and extreme abundance exist, the greed in abundance that allows the poverty is sin, but as abundance has increased that sin has decreased. As wealthy people like Warren Buffett and Bill Gates become more an more generous, extreme poverty is rapidly decreasing.

Although this is debatable, I believe even human sinfulness is also decreasing. Christians are in the habit of creating sinfulness hierarchies that evolve when new sins begin to annoy Christians more than old sins, but our chosen hierarchy shouldn't trump Jesus' hierarchy. Jesus was graceful and patient with prostitutes, thieves, and murderers, but he had little patience for the actions of the judgmental and prideful religious leaders. There is an earthiness to the sins of the people Jesus surrounded himself with. They were sins of the flesh. The sins Jesus criticized most were spiritual and relational sins. The sins of those he called vipers were sins of judgment, separation, and unbelief.

Self-righteousness, judgmentalism, and guilt-mongering are sins that disguise themselves as virtues. They are driven by pride and a selfish need for justice, but they claim holy motivations. When we unleash anger on the sins of others, we feel religious. When we judge the addictions of others, we diminish the sins that tempt us. When we are on the lookout for anything that resembles sin, hoping to justify our prediction of decline, we create new sins out of actions that are little more than unhealthy habits. If Christians will watch for things that are good and worthy of praise, they will see goodness is increasing. They will see there are people all over the world who have found joy in service, who have begun the long process of removing unhealthy habits from their lives, who have discovered revolutionary ways to help more people with less effort, and who regularly sacrifice for the good of others. Cable television and the internet make sin look more frequent, but the reporting of sin is actually evidence of sins decline. As the world becomes more aware of sin, humanity fights against the most egregious sins. There will always be a list of most egregious sins, but it appears

26. Wang, "Poverty in Numbers," para. 9.

to me that sin has decreased so much that it has now reached a comprehensible, or at least a reportable, level.

Slavery, for example, was an accepted practice for most of history, but no more. For most of history, when a nation wanted to get land from another nation, they killed people to take it; now land is acquired through purchases. Alliances of nations have held warlords and powerful thugs at bay. Violent gangsters and pirates still exist, but society has joined together to fight against them rather than let them terrorize as long as they don't hurt us. Sexism and racism have declined at a rate never seen before, and human rights violations are mostly tame compared to past atrocities. Practices such as human sacrifice and other sexual and violent pagan rituals have all but disappeared, and worldwide crime rates are plummeting.[27]

I am inclined to say the greatest areas of sinfulness the world allows today are abortion and sexual infidelity, yet even abortion rates in much of the world are declining,[28] and sexual infidelity has been rampant throughout human history. It is not unique to the time in which we live. In much of the world, prostitution is now illegal, and polygamy is detested. When an increasing number of sins are outlawed at the same time that crime rates decrease, there is plenty of reason to believe sin is decreasing. Admittedly, this is a difficult argument to make because humans will always be sinful. There will always be sins that people can point to to justify their cynicism, but it requires a great leap in logic to conclude the world is not becoming less sinful in at least some of the areas that have brought so much pain to the world in the past.

Gloomy Church

Hebrews 13:17 instructs pastors to do their work "with joy and not with groaning, for that would be of no advantage to you." This verse led John Piper to say, "A gloomy pastor makes a sick congregation."[29] Apocalyptic predications based on the current state of the church ignores over 1,000 years of Christian history in the Near East. Piper goes on to say, "An alarmist approach to eschatology is usually historically naïve."[30] Each eschatological theory has sufficient theological capacity to provide room for optimism for

27. Pinker, *Better Angels of Our Nature*, 1.

28. Levy, "Abortion Rates," para. 1.

29. Piper, "Gospel Hope for Cultural Pessimists," para. 10.

30. Piper, "Gospel Hope for Cultural Pessimists," para. 4.

the future of the church to govern their activity until the second coming of Christ, but some theologies do so with more dedication. All holistic views of the Bible recognize evil will not triumph, but some doom Christianity to decline until the triumph is realized. Dispensationalism has a tendency to turns God's infinite story into a finite game with a reward at the end for the winner.

Harold Eberle writes,

> Most of the great leaders throughout Church history held to a victorious eschatology. However, during the twentieth century, Christians became increasingly skeptical and pessimistic about the future . . . As the world was thrust face-to-face with challenges and the wickedness of war, people embraced a negative view of humanity and a pessimistic view of the future. It was during those trying periods when many Christians embraced a more pessimistic eschatology. They came to believe that the world is gradually slipping under the influence of wicked leaders and eventually Satan will take control of the economic and religious systems of the world.[31]

As the world experiences a widespread increase in anxiety, Christians hold the keys to the hope the world so desperately needs. Hope, and the positivity it brings, is central to Christian methods and purpose.

Documentational Scripture

The passages that point to specific events in time—we'll call them documentational passages—can be logically divided into two categories: history and prophecy. Documentational passages that are history have already happened. Documentational passages that are prophecy have not yet happened. However, there is much disagreement about which passages fall into which category, because prophecy that has been fulfilled, whether recently or in antiquity, becomes history.[32] Most of the prophecies in Scripture have already been fulfilled,[33] therefore, an examination of biblical history will aid in understanding those passages that are often considered to be unfulfilled prophecies.[34]

31. Eberle and Trench, *Victorious Eschatology*, 217.

32. Wilson, *Heaven Misplaced*, 93.

33. Sproul, *Last Days*, 47.

34. Wilson, *Heaven Misplaced*, 16.

Consider this optimistic prophecy of Jesus Christ that points to the success of the church, not to the demise of the world, as a sign of his return. In Matthew 23, Jesus tells the people of Jerusalem that because they rejected the Christian prophets, their house would be left "desolate" until they proclaim, "Blessed is he who comes in the name of the Lord" (Matt 23:37–39). The word "house" here could either refer to the whole polity of Israel or to the temple, but either way the Jews[35] would become followers of Christ before he returns. This most certainly has not happened on a large scale. Paul often began his ministry in a city at the synagogue, and after he was rejected by the Jews, the gentiles were drawn to his message. Paul believed the conversion of the gentiles would arouse "envy" in the Jews that would result in the Jews accepting Christ (Rom 11:14). Perhaps this will happen on a large scale when the nations turn to God.

Left behind theology requires the temple to be rebuilt so the antichrist can take control of it and destroy it again. The nation of Israel would love to rebuild the temple. In fact, they are prepared to do so as soon as they can, but the death of Jesus was meant to end the Jewish sacrificial system. The curtain was torn, but the Jewish people quickly repaired it and resumed animal sacrifices. Christians who support the recommencement of animal sacrifice detract from the impact of Christ's sacrifice.

The focus of many biblical prophecies is the nation of Israel—its birth, development, rebellion, destruction, and redemption—but all prophecies at least partially point to Jesus. A messenger spoke to John, saying, "Worship God! For the testimony of Jesus is the spirit of prophecy" (Rev 19:10). This is prophecy, to tell of Jesus and his kingdom, but prophecy "will become useless . . . Now our knowledge is partial and incomplete, and even the gift of prophecy reveals only part of the whole picture!" (1 Cor 13:8–9). Therefore, the focus of prophecy is not a detailed description of endtime predictions of a tribulation (suffering resulting from persecution), a millennium (the 1,000-year period referenced in Rev 20), or even a rapture (the moment all Christians will physically join Jesus Christ for eternity), but on a King and his kingdom. Although much of biblical prophecy has already happened, the expansion of this kingdom is proceeding. It is at hand, continuing, and near. Matthew 3:2 is one of many passages that say, "the kingdom of heaven has come near."[36] It is a mistake to assume we are at

---

35. Sproul, *Last Days*, 60.

36. Other passages with similar statements include Matt 4:17; 10:7; 12:28, Mark 1:15; Luke 10:9–11; 11:20.

the end of this kingdom development and growth, but Christians have been making that assumption for centuries.[37]

The kingdom has been steadily growing since the day of Christ, and yet many Christians continue to look for a future kingdom, choosing to focus on the kingdom as a future reality rather than a present reality. Kingdom growth is happening now, exactly as Jesus promised it would. Just as nothing can stop the chemical reaction taking place when yeast is introduced into flour, nothing can stop the growth of the church (Gal 5:9). This line of reasoning could lead theologians to much more optimistic conclusions, and, as they begin to believe success is possible, optimism will produce positive results.

THE REACH OF DISPENSATIONALISM

In showing how premillennialism and political posturing are often linked, Dr. John Fea, a historian and evangelical Christian, writes,

> Because religion in America directly impacts policy, military leaders and planners must learn to recognize the tenets and implications of American millennial thought. Millennialism has always been a feature of the American culture and has shaped not only the objectives of U.S. government policy, but also the way in which we interpret the words and actions of other actors on the international stage . . . Pessimism and paranoia are two possible results of premillennial influence.[38]

After pointing out that pessimism and paranoia may result from premillennial influence, John Fea writes that the effects of premillennialism are so engrained in American Christianity that America's adversaries can use dispensational interpretations of prophecy to predict the future actions of America's military.[39] Major Brian L. Stuckert agrees with this assessment when he writes, "Since the beginning of the Republic, various forms of millennial religious doctrines, of which dispensational premillennialism is the most recent, have shaped U.S. national security strategy."[40]

---

37. Wilson, *Heaven Misplaced*, 82.

38. Fea, "Strategic Implications of American Millennialism," para. 6.

39. Fea, "Strategic Implications of American Millennialism," para. 8.

40. Stuckert, "Strategic Implications of American Millennialism," 1.

On RedState.com, Erick Erickson, a politically active Christian who is a premillennialist, admits his eschatological beliefs made him pessimistic about the future of the church and cynical about the people in the church:

> On the last day there will be a narrow gate. That makes me pessimistic about my future in politics and the future voices on the right . . . In the 1800's [stet] with the rise of the Great Awakening, students of eschatology viewed the end times rather favorably. The whole world would come to Christ, many of them thought. I view the end times more pessimistically. I think there'll be many more through the pearly gates than I want, but a whole lot less than I expect.[41]

Dr. Joel McDurmon argues with the assertion made by Erick Erickson in an article titled "An Open Letter to Erick Erickson: Reason to Dump the Pessimistic Eschatology." McDurmon says,

> Thank you, RedState.com mogul Erick Erickson, for showing us clearly the soft underbelly of the mainstream Christian right in America: pessimistic eschatology. I, and others, have of course said this for some time now. You have now exposed it openly, and have admitted that your eschatology dictates general hopelessness in your considerable political activism.[42]

In *Purity, Power, and Pentecostal Light*, Christopher Jon Bransletter compares the impact eschatology had on the optimism for revival of two revivalists, Aaron M. Hills and Reuben A. Torrey.[43] Hills was a postmillennialist. Torrey was a dispensationalist. The difference in their eschatological beliefs is the most impactful of their theological differences. The optimistic view of history, the church, and the gospel that characterizes most postmillennialists "could not be any farther from the dispensationalist's negative attitude toward the same."[44] That is just the beginning of the differences these two eschatological beliefs produce, from social reform and integration to larger doctrinal and strategic commitments. Eschatology reveals itself as more than a secondary doctrine for revivalists. It drives them to push toward widespread, long-term success, or settle for incomplete accomplishments. A Christian's eschatology is a major contributor to his or

41. Erickson, "I Increasingly Find Conflict," para. 8.
42. McDurmon, "Open Letter to Erick Erickson," para. 5.
43. Branstetter, *Purity, Power, and Pentecostal Light*, 209.
44. Branstetter, *Purity, Power, and Pentecostal Light*, 205.

her mission and plays a key role in developing his attitude toward pre-Christians. Hills writes, in a statement that seems to sufficiently predict his success as a Christian evangelist, "Jesus never spoke one syllable about the insufficiency of the Holy Spirit and the gospel, and the present means of grace to win the world and establish his kingdom. He never intimated that . . . all these Christian instrumentalities were never intended to succeed! God inaugurated these means and they will succeed!"[45]

If the world is a burning apartment building that cannot be saved, the evangelist will work to save as many people as possible before the danger of collapse becomes too great. If a firefighter operates under the assumption the fire will be victorious, he begins to create a hierarchy, relegating some of the people in the building as a lost cause and others as worth the effort. If the firefighter operates under the belief the flames are contained and receding, he or she may be so bold as to believe every person in the building can be saved and work to accomplish that goal no matter how close to the fire each person is. Some in the American Christian church have been blinded by a theology that has led to a contemptuous view of the future. This pessimistic theology has led to a Christianity that shields itself from imminent danger, a Zionist theology that is overly militant and political, and a selectivism theology that leads to judgmentalism and eventually deems certain individuals as lost causes. About the impact of dispensationalism on a person's ideas, Dr. Tommy Ice writes, "Dispensationalism made sense to many Calvinists who were pessimistic about individual human nature and it followed that society as a whole was in the same condition."[46]

When religious leaders teach the world that the end is coming, they encourage an attitude of peril. Gary DeMar writes,

> What impact does antichrist speculation have on the ideological battles we are fighting today? If the antichrist is alive and well on planet earth, and the signs of the last day are all around us, then why bother with education, politics, the media, international affairs, economics, and a whole host of other worldview issues? . . . In time, the activists throw up their hands and follow the path of prophetic logic: If all the signs point to the near return of Jesus, and all sorts of bad things are going to happen, including an economic meltdown like the one described by prophecy writers John Hagee (Financial Armageddon) and David Jeremiah (The Coming

---

45. Hills, *Fundamental Christian Theology*, 354.

46. Ice, "Short History of Dispensationalism," para. 59.

Economic Armageddon), then why spend my time and resources trying to fight something that is inevitable?[47]

Urgency

Postmillennialism leads to a narrative more prone to social activism, but premillennial dispensationalism leads adherents to disconnection from society. Eschatological differences are better defined as differences in overarching vision than in systematic doctrine.[48] In practice, their social attitudes are completely different. To illustrate, Donald W. Dayton points out that postmillennialists founded liberal arts colleges, but dispensationalists founded Bible colleges. He notes, "The Bible school has no place for the study of history, literature, philosophy, science, etc. because these have no real role other than distractions in the premillennialist agenda. The urgency of the imminence of the return of Christ requires the minimum of biblical training and the equipping of the student in practical ministries."[49] His assertion that there is no place for these things in the Bible school may be an overstatement, but his point is well taken. Liberal arts universities, like optimistic eschatologists, produce individuals who invest in the future of society, develop comprehensive strategies of success, and recognize the fusion of their spiritual and physical lives.

This is not to say urgency is a bad thing; it is important that Christians act with urgency. It is the only way we will win people to Christ. Penn Jillette, a famous atheist and member of the Penn and Teller magic team, often says that even though he doesn't believe in God, he doesn't respect Christians who don't proselytize. If Christians believe people who aren't Christians are destined to suffer for eternity in hell, how could they not spend every moment of their lives telling people how to be saved? Urgency is not only necessary, it is an obvious response to the gospel.

I am a huge fan of escape rooms. I have done escape rooms all over the country, and one of the many important lessons I have learned is the importance of urgency. An escape room is a themed room that people pay to get locked in, and they are given one hour to escape. Every room is different, but there is a series of clues, puzzles, locks, and doors a team must

---

47. DeMar, "Why Bother?," para. 19.

48. Branstetter, *Purity, Power, and Pentecostal Light*, 206.

49. Dayton, *Methodism & the Fragmentation of American Protestantism*, 11.

complete/open in order to escape. If a team spends too much time on a puzzle, they won't have enough time to complete future puzzles. If you get stuck, it's important to ask for a hint before you have wasted too much time. Teams that take their time and forget that the clock is always moving, will fail to escape in time. One hour is enough time that people often forget to keep moving quickly forward, but there is also a danger in moving too quickly. If a team moves rapidly through the puzzle that is directly in front of them and neglects the other clues around them or fails to compile materials, tools, or resources for future puzzles, their urgency will actually cause them to fail.

The same is true about our Christian responsibility. We must stay focused on the short time we have on this earth to lead people to Christ, but that does not mean investing in long-game strategies is a waste of time. We must not allow urgency to make us focus our efforts on those people who can be most easily and quickly led to Christ and neglect those people who will only be won after we invest in them for a lifetime, and we must not neglect the investments that will ensure there are optimistic Christians around to disciple our grandkids.

DISCUSSION QUESTIONS:

a. What are some of the effects of negative theology? Do you think there are any involuntary responses to those beliefs?

b. Why do you think God told John not to write down the revelation he saw in Revelation 10? In what areas of our lives should we learn to have restraint?

c. Have you read the *Left Behind* books? What do you think of them?

d. Why are people drawn to apocalyptic predictions?

6

Biblical Eschatology

The people of God live precisely between the ascension and the return. In the meantime, God's people are joined to Jesus Christ by the Spirit and, while God's people wait, they are commanded to remain in faith, hope, and love.[1]

—ED LOVE

CHRISTIANS SHOULD NOT PUT their faith in an interpretation of end-times prophecies, but it can be helpful to understand the range of interpretations theologians have developed. For that reason, this chapter will provide a concise survey of those prophecies. We will do that by looking at some of those portions of the Bible that refer to the second coming of Jesus Christ. The purpose of this chapter is not to advocate for a specific eschatological theory. Instead, it will provide an interpretation of some of the crucial Bible passages that speak of eschatology and demonstrate that no single interpretation of these passages can be trusted with absolute confidence.

Isaiah 46:10 tells us God has made known the end from the beginning. Does that mean we can know what will happen at the end of time? Yes, but not in the way an individual knows a clock will chime on the hour. Rather the end is known similar to the way a mother knows she would sacrifice everything for her child. We have not, and will not, know the *date* of the end of time, but we do know the *result* of the end.

1. Love, "Coming God," 52.

This book will assume two areas of general agreement. The first is that a second coming of Christ is imminent. The second assumed agreement is no man can know the day of Jesus' return. The temptation to use enigmatic prophecies[2] to predict the exact date of Jesus' return has caused many smart people to look ignorant.[3]

EXAMINATION OF DOCUMENTATIONAL SCRIPTURE

Prophecies of Isaiah

Isaiah demonstrated an optimistic form of semiotics that displayed faith in God's sovereignty in the future despite the gloomy time in which he lived. The prophecies in Isaiah are largely focused on the Jewish plight of future enslavement by the Babylonians and their eventual deliverance, but it also points, like other prophetic books, to a future Messiah and introduces gentiles to God's salvation narrative. When Isaiah 28:5 speaks of a great day that is coming, it appears to be a glorious day of Jesus' reign with his people: "In that day the Lord Almighty will be a glorious crown, a beautiful wreath for the remnant of his people." Isaiah's focus was lifted from the dark days that faced his beloved people to a future time when glory would come upon the earth.[4]

There is no mention in the book of Isaiah of a tribulation, a millennium, the decline of the kingdom, a constant increase of the oppression of the church, or a third coming of Jesus Christ. Instead, Isaiah 46:10 paints an optimistic picture of those end times: "I make known the end from the beginning, from ancient times, what is still to come. I say, 'My purpose will stand, and I will do all that I please.'" The dread that is so often the central idea of eschatological discussions cannot be justified by the book of Isaiah or similar books of prophecy. The prophetic books of the Bible "are concerned primarily with this life rather than anything beyond it," and the few passages that do reference the afterlife are "unclear."[5]

2. Sproul, *Last Days*, 68.

3. Sproul, *Last Days*, 52.

4. See also Isa 11:10; 31:7.

5. Boda and McConville, *Dictionary of the Old Testament*, 1.

Paul quotes another messianic prophecy from the book of Isaiah when he writes, "The Root of Jesse will spring up, one who will arise to rule over the nations; in him the gentiles will hope" (Rom 15:12–14). The passage being quoted is Isaiah 11:6–10, which points to an almost too-good-to-be-true future time dispensationalists associate with a time after the second coming of Jesus. The passage in Isaiah talks about an incredible time of peace when many people will turn to Jesus. Douglas Wilson is a postmillennialist, someone who believes all of the Bible was written before AD 70 and that most of the prophecies Bible scholars consider eschatological actually point to the events surrounding the destruction of the Jerusalem temple by Nero. As a historical optimist, Douglas Wilson wrote this about that passage in Romans, "The great apostle Paul is appealing to Isaiah as a justification for his preaching to the gentiles. And since then, we have had two thousand years of the Lord's government and peace increasing."[6]

Prophecies of Daniel

The book of Daniel also predicts the coming of the Messiah. When Daniel interpreted King Nebuchadnezzar's dream, he spoke of empires that would come over the next several centuries. Those empires seem to have been the empires of Babylon (Nebuchadnezzar's kingdom), Persia, Greece, and Rome. The final portion of the dream concerned a fifth kingdom that would be set up during the fourth. It was compared to a "rock cut out" by divine hands that would strike the other kingdoms and crush them to pieces (Dan 2:45). What is the fifth kingdom? Is this the kingdom Jesus repeatedly described while he was on Earth? Daniel's explanation gives us a strong indication it is: "In the time of those kings, the God of heaven will set up a kingdom that will never be destroyed, nor will it be left to another people" (Dan 2:44). This seems to parallel Jesus' own words that the "gates of Hades will not overcome [the church]" (Matt 16:18). If the Christian church now operates in this kingdom, this prophesy should be a great source of biblical optimism about the church's future.

The Jews seem to have missed it because they were looking for a political kingdom, but Jesus told Pilate his kingdom was not of this world (John 18:36). This explanation convinced Pilate Jesus was a king (John 18:37). Jesus' mission cannot be separated from his kingdom.[7] To assume a rapture

6. Wilson, *Heaven Misplaced*, 16.

7. Riddlebarger, *Case for Amillennialism*, 102.

of the saints will occur, followed by a great tribulation upon this earth and a royal reign of the Christians, followed by the final judgment, is to fall into Pilate's trap.[8] The kingdom is not an earthly, political kingdom.[9]

The disciples apparently knew Christ would return. They said, "When will all this happen? What sign will signal your return and the end of the world?" (Matt 24:3). Douglas Wilson points out this statement implies the two events—the return of Christ and the end of the world—will occur at the same time.[10] As the disciples watched Jesus ascend to heaven, two men in white robes, presumably angels, asked them, "Why are you standing here staring into heaven? Jesus has been taken from you into heaven, but someday he will return from heaven in the same way you saw him go!" (Acts 1:11). This implies the second coming of Jesus will be just that, a coming to earth,[11] not a taking away from earth.[12]

Daniel wrote this about that kingdom:

> In my vision at night I looked, and there before me was one like a son of man, coming with the clouds of heaven. He approached the Ancient of Days and was led into his presence. He was given authority, glory and sovereign power; all peoples, nations and men of every language worshiped him. His dominion is an everlasting dominion that will not pass away, and his kingdom is one that will never be destroyed. (Dan 7:13–14)

Jesus claimed to be the fulfillment of this prophecy when he said, "All authority in heaven and on earth has been given to me" (Matt 28:18), and according to Daniel 7:14, his dominion will never be destroyed.[13]

According to 1 Corinthians 15:19, if our only hope is the kingdom in this age, we have no hope at all. Matthew 11:12 implies the kingdom was in existence in the past; Mark 10:15 implies we can receive the kingdom in this life; and Luke 16:16 implies it is coming. Jesus seemed to imply the kingdom would not come dramatically, but it would expand slowly. In Matthew 13:31, Jesus compares the kingdom to a seed that takes time to grow, and in verse 33 to yeast that was mixed into a large amount of flour,

8. See also Luke 17:20 and John 3:3.

9. Riddlebarger, *Case for Amillennialism*, 107.

10. Wilson, *Heaven Misplaced, 106.*

11. Wilson, *Heaven Misplaced*, 21.

12. For more acknowledgments of the second coming, see Matt 24:30; John 14:3; 1 Thess 4:16; Heb 9:8; Jas 5:8; 2 Pet 3:10; 1 John 3:23; Rev 1:7; 22:20.

13. Wilson, *Heaven Misplaced*, 103.

implying a slow renovation of the dough (Matt 13:31–33).[14] The kingdom of God was said to be at hand, but also near. Seemingly, it is here but not yet fully here. If the kingdom was a present reality when Luke 17:20–21 was written, the kingdom is a past and future reality.[15]

After Jesus' resurrection from the dead, his followers inquired, "Lord, are you at this time going to restore the kingdom to Israel?" (Acts 1:6). Christ did not give them a "yes" or a "no." Instead he told them there was work to do and power to do it with (Acts 1:7–8).

Sevens

Daniel 9:24–27 is a metaphorical passage that predicts a stop to the temple sacrificial system. Daniel 9:25 says, "From the time the word goes out to restore and rebuild Jerusalem until the Anointed One, the ruler, comes, there will be seven 'sevens,' and sixty-two 'sevens.'" Most commentators agree the seven "sevens" cover the period of the rebuilding of the city in the days of Ezra and Nehemiah, and the sixty-two "sevens" span the time from the end of the rebuilding to some period of time in the life of Christ. Daniel 9:26–27 says, "After the sixty-two 'sevens,' the Anointed One will be put to death and will have nothing. The people of the ruler who will come will destroy the city and the sanctuary. The end will come like a flood: War will continue until the end, and desolations have been decreed. He will confirm a covenant with many for one 'seven.' In the middle of the 'seven' he will put an end to sacrifice and offering." Many Amillennialists, Postmillennialists, and Historic Premillennialists simply connect the final 'seven' to the death of Christ and the destruction of the temple by Nero and the Roman General Titus in AD 70. Dispensationalists add time (the church age) to the prophesy between the sixty-ninth and seventieth "seven." They believe the seventieth "seven" will happen in the future. Therefore, Dispensationalists believe a rapture of Christians will occur when Jesus secretly returns to earth at the beginning of the seventieth "seven."

14. See also Mark 4:25–29, 30–32.
15. Piper, "Is the Kingdom Present or Future?," para. 3.

The Beast

The beast and abomination spoken of in Daniel 9:27 and Revelation 13 can be interpreted as metaphorical, someone who existed in the past, or someone who will exist in the future. The primary marking of the beast's existence is the end of temple sacrifice (Dan 9:27). Some people connect the beast's arrival to a future destruction of the temple. Some point to the destruction of the temple in AD 70, but even if the beast brings about a great tribulation in the future, right before or right after the second coming of Jesus, the prophecies that are used to predict that do not foretell a constant decline of the church until that happens.

Prophecies of Timothy and Titus

Second Timothy 3:1–5 says,

> But mark this: There will be terrible times in the last days. People will be lovers of themselves, lovers of money, boastful, proud, abusive, disobedient to their parents, ungrateful, unholy, without love, unforgiving, slanderous, without self-control, brutal, not lovers of the good, treacherous, rash, conceited, lovers of pleasure rather than lovers of God—having a form of godliness but denying its power. Have nothing to do with such people.

Paul shows Timothy that the signs of living in the "last times" are already to be seen in the activity of false teachers who peddle heresy for material gain and for illicit encounters with "silly women," but Paul assures Timothy the opposition will amount to nothing.[16]

It would be a mistake to use a passage like 2 Timothy 3:1–5 to justify pessimistic expectations by interpreting it as a description of a world that will forever be in moral and physical decline. There is no statement of escalation of trouble explicitly written in 2 Timothy. If the last days began in the time of Jesus, the terrible times described could be contained to a period in the last days or consistent until the return of Christ. It is at least possible the perils described in 2 Timothy 3 will decrease.[17]

Paul writes the book of 2 Timothy from prison in the midst of circumstances that would lead most people to thoughts of extreme pessimism about the future, in a time that could literally be described as his last days

---

16. DeSilva, *Introduction to the New Testament*, 735.

17. Sproul, *Last Days*, 200.

in this world. It was also written in a time when Nero persecuted Christians on a staggering level, using gladiators and wild animals to slaughter Christians in arenas. Such behavior would never be tolerated today as it was in the first century.[18] In this letter, Paul describes the sinful people of his day as "sinful people in an era in history."[19]

The description of sinful behavior and dire circumstances in 2 Timothy 3 could just as easily point to Timothy's world as to ours, if not more so. Other New Testament letters use similar language to point out similar behavior in the first century.[20] The Greek present tense used in that passage does imply the verb is present and moving forward, but in this case, William Mounce, addressing the present tense of Paul's language, argues that 2 Timothy 3:5 "shows that while the vice list may be applied to society in general, Paul is really thinking about certain people professing to be Christians."[21] The Wycliffe Commentary points out "The last days probably is not here limited to the eschatological age-end, but includes the Gnostic attack of the church then developing."[22] Although we are not given a full prophecy of what will happen in the entirety of the last days, we can see conditions have not declined steadily since the time of Jesus.

The arrival of Jesus Christ marked the beginning of the end. "We've now had about 2,000 years of last days. That's roughly equal to the time between Abraham and Jesus—beginning at God's first covenant agreement with humanity, through Abraham, and reaching to the start of his second covenant, through Jesus."[23] Speaking of Jesus, 1 Peter 1:20 says, "He was chosen before the creation of the world, but was revealed in these last times for your sake." 1 John 2:18 says, "Dear children, this is the last hour; and as you have heard that the antichrist is coming, even now many antichrists have come. This is how we know it is the last hour." The evil that is described in these passages is meant to describe the world in which we already live.

The logical mind then seeks to determine if Scripture implies the horrible times described therein will get worse in the latter part of the last days. Even though the church has often been resilient, prophetic warnings of persecution, evil behavior, and natural disaster can have a crippling effect

18. EyeWitness to History, "Nero Persecutes the Christians," para. 4.

19. Miller, *Complete Guide to the Bible*, 449.

20. Mounce, *Pastoral Epistles*, 547. Also, see Acts 20:29–30 and Titus 1:10–13.

21. Mounce, *Pastoral Epistles*, 547.

22. Pfeiffer and Harrison, *Wycliffe Bible Commentary*, 1387.

23. Miller, *Complete Guide to the Bible*, 449.

on the subject of pain if the imagination allows them to grow to an infinite height. How great will the suffering become if the pain will increase until the second advent? If the suffering can only increase, it is tempting to hope for the second coming before Christians accomplish all they can to win as many people as possible.

If the dispensationalist claims suffering will increase until Christ's second coming, the current reality of Christianity in the United States seems to disprove that theory. It requires a great watering down of the word "suffer" to imply all Christians in America face persecution. And to dismiss the postmillennialist's interpretation of Scripture due to a lack of Christian suffering during the rise of Christianity is overstating the Bible's warnings of suffering.

Prophecies of Revelation

G. K. Chesterton writes, "Though St. John the Evangelist saw many strange monsters in his vision, he saw no creature so wild as one of his own commentators."[24] John's Revelation was a letter to seven churches, and its readers would be wise to read it with a full understanding of who the letter was written to.[25] Some theologians convincingly connect those seven churches to seven stages of Christian history. That requires more guessing, stretching, and reading between the lines than I am willing to do here, but there are some undeniable similarities between the seven churches and some of the events in church history.

John's wild and fantastic images encourage Christians in Asia Minor to persevere through the trials they are facing. When the book of Revelation depicts wrath, it is primarily referring to the future wrath of God on the devil, his forces, or those who were unfaithful to God.[26] Examples of these references include a statement in 6:16–17 about the "wrath of the Lamb that is to fall upon the kings of the earth," a statement in 14:10 of an angel who threatens "anyone who worships the beast," and a statement in 11:18 about God's wrath on those who were "destroying the earth."[27] Much of the letter is written about the hope offered to those who are rescued by the Lamb that was crucified and raised from the dead. This truth relegates

24. Chesterton, *Orthodoxy*, 8.

25. DeSilva, *Introduction to the New Testament*, 889.

26. Martin and Davids, *Dictionary of the Later New Testament*, 1239.

27. Martin and Davids, *Dictionary of the Later New Testament*, 1239–40.

the coming wrath and destruction to those who "shrink back" from the faith, while those who "have faith" will be saved (Heb 10:39).

Revelation is not a detailed, step-by-step description of what will happen in the future. It is more like a movie trailer. If you try to figure out what every image and statement means, you'll start stretching to make connections that just aren't there to make. Have you ever watched a Marvel movie trailer with a nerd? I have. One of my best friends, Chris, can watch a Marvel movie trailer and get so much more out of it than I can. I hear an epic soundtrack, get a short glimpse a bunch of cool action scenes, and take note of the main characters that will be in the movie. Chris on the other hand can tell me the background of the villain of the movie. He can understand why things happen before they happen by looking at the context of the scene clips, but there are parts of Marvel movie previews that even Chris can't understand because he hasn't been given enough context. The book of Revelation is like a movie trailer. With some education, you can learn more about it, but there are some details we just can't understand until we see the movie.

The date the book of Revelation was written plays a key role in the interpretation of its predictions. The book was either written before AD 70 or in the 90s AD. The evidence of a late writing is largely based on a reference in the writing of Irenaeus, a student of Polycarp. Polycarp was a disciple of John, the author of Revelation. Irenaeus was born in AD 130, but he wrote the book *Against Heresies* in AD 180. In that book, he wrote about John's revelation as having been already written at the close of the reign of Domitian.[28] Domitian died in AD 96.[29] You can do with that what you will, but I have a hard time putting much confidence in that vague reference.

The New Testament has a tone of urgency and expectation that seems to point to an event that will come soon. This leads premillennialists and amillennialists to argue the authors of the New Testament were misunderstanding the prophesies of Jesus and the prophets when they used the word "soon." Douglas Wilson writes that most of the authors of the New Testament seem to be "waiting for something drastic that will happen soon, and not one of them even mentions the most cataclysmic event in Jewish history—the fall of Jerusalem in AD 70—as being past. That event was the destruction of the old Judaic order and its replacement by the Christian

28. Sproul, *Last Days*.

29. Jackson, "When Was the Book of Revelation Written?," para. 5.

church, the New Israel."[30] One would assume those events would have been referenced if a book was written after AD 70. This seems to be an obvious argument for an early authorship of Revelation.

Were the Bible's authors confused when they used the word "soon" (see Matt 24:34, Rom 13:12–14, Rev 1:1)? Christians who believe these documentational passages refer to events that will happen in the future donate an argument to skeptics of the Bible who argue the authors were proven wrong when the prophesied events didn't occur. Christians who believe the prophesied events were fulfilled in AD 70 or at some other time in history are more equipped to defend the authors.

Daniel was told to seal the words of a prophecy because the prophesied event was far in the future, and he was only 400 years from the prophesy's fulfillment (Dan 12:4). Revelation 22:10 told the prophet not to seal up the words of the prophecy because the time was near. It appears the events prophesied in Revelation would take place less than 400 years after the book was written.

Revelation 6:9 talks of souls who had been martyred for being faithful to their testimony, using similar language as those who are beheaded because of their testimony in Revelation 20. The people who are beheaded in Revelation 20:4 are beheaded by the seven-headed beast from 12:3. Postmillennialists argue the seven heads of the beast point to the same thing to which the seven hills and seven kings point—Nero. Nero persecuted the church from AD 64 to AD 68—for 42 months, as described in Revelation 13:5–7.

The premillennialist interpretation concludes that every unbeliever was killed in Revelation 19, but Revelation 20 refers to Satan deceiving the nations. If all the people were destroyed in Revelation 19, who is left to compose the nations in Revelation 20, and who will be deceived? It would seem logical to conclude Revelation 19 and 20 use different imagery to predict the same event: the second coming of Christ. If that is true, it would also seem logical to conclude the 1,000-year reign could just as likely be a heavenly or spiritual reign as an earthly reign.

Prophecies of Thessalonians

First Corinthians 15:15–58 shows the death of death (the termination of physical death) occurs at the second coming of Jesus. No man will die a

30. Wilson, *Heaven Misplaced*, 111.

physical death after Jesus returns to earth. Similarly, the glorification of Christians and the redemption of the world will occur simultaneously with Jesus' return. Romans 8:18–23 shows that when the sons of God are revealed at the second coming of Jesus, all of creation will be redeemed. The curse cannot perpetuate beyond the second advent. There is also no evidence individuals will have the ability to come to a saving faith in Jesus Christ after the second coming of Jesus. Second Thessalonians 1:5–8 gives evidence of these things happening when Christ returns:

> And God will use this persecution to show his justice and to make you worthy of his kingdom, for which you are suffering. In his justice he will pay back those who persecute you. And God will provide rest for you who are being persecuted and also for us when the Lord Jesus appears from heaven. He will come with his mighty angels, in flaming fire, bringing judgment on those who don't know God and on those who refuse to obey the Good News of our Lord Jesus.

Matthew 13 contains multiple verses that indicate "the judgment will occur at the time of our Lord's return."[31] This produces much difficulty for premillennialists, who claim there will be a literal 1,000-year period between Jesus' return and the final judgment. In Matthew 13:40–43, Jesus says,

> As the weeds are pulled up and burned in the fire, so it will be at the end of the age. The Son of Man will send out his angels, and they will weed out of his kingdom everything that causes sin and all who do evil. They will throw them into the blazing furnace, where there will be weeping and gnashing of teeth. Then the righteous will shine like the sun in the kingdom of their Father. Whoever has ears, let them hear.

Kim Riddlebarger argues "premillennialists must attempt to sidestep the clear teaching of Scripture that the resurrection (1 Cor 15:35–57, 1 Thess 4:13—5:11, 2 Thess 1:5–10), the restoration of all things (2 Pet 3:3–15), and the judgment occur at the same time—our Lord's second advent."[32]

The Scripture passage that will likely be used to argue against the idea of positive Christianity is 1 Thessalonians 5:1–8, which says,

---

31. Riddlebarger, *Case for Amillennialism*, 85.

32. Riddlebarger, *Case for Amillennialism*, 86.

Now, brothers and sisters, about times and dates we do not need to write to you, for you know very well that the day of the Lord will come like a thief in the night. While people are saying, "Peace and safety," destruction will come on them suddenly, as labor pains on a pregnant woman, and they will not escape. But you, brothers and sisters, are not in darkness so that this day should surprise you like a thief. You are all children of the light and children of the day. We do not belong to the night or to the darkness. So then, let us not be like others, who are asleep, but let us be awake and sober. For those who sleep, sleep at night, and those who get drunk, get drunk at night. But since we belong to the day, let us be sober, putting on faith and love as a breastplate, and the hope of salvation as a helmet.

This passage has been used by some theologians to argue for a secret rapture of Christians before the tribulation. This passage has been used to argue the world will become increasingly sinful and Christian positivity is the "peace and safety" that will bring destruction, but Paul was not saying peace and safety will cause destruction. He was saying the destruction will come when people are experiencing peace and safety. Postmillennialists say the destruction reference in verse 3 was the destruction of the temple in AD 70. Premillennialists say the destruction will happen in the future before the second coming of Christ, but whichever is right, this verse does not speak of a rapture. It could be speaking of the second coming of Christ because 1 Thessalonians 4 does broach that subject, and Paul did not include chapter separations in his writing. It is very difficult to insert a rapture of Christians before the second coming of Christ into this passage, but that is what dispensationalism does. This passage is an exhortation to missional urgency and focus, or it is a documentation of the warning Christians received about the events that occurred in AD 70.

Increase of Wickedness

Writers such as Alan E. Kurschner and Steve Hays offer a defense of premillennialism that points to Matthew 24:12–13 as proof that wickedness will continually increase.[33] That passage says, "Because of the increase of wickedness, the love of most will grow cold, but the one who stands firm to the end will be saved." This passage does not speak of the extent to which

33. Kurschner, "Randal Rauser Asserts," para. 7.

the wickedness will increase or for how long it will continue to increase. Mortal men can only attempt to compare the intensity of wickedness to the past, and that gives very little insight into the heights it could reach. This is a vague reference to hang a theology on. In fact, that passage goes on to say, "For then there will be great distress, unequaled from the beginning of the world until now—and never to be equaled again" (Matt 24:21). And if that verse is referring to the destruction of the temple in AD 70, it should encourage readers that peace will continue to increase.

Douglas Wilson argues that the series of troubles cited in passages like these "are not talking about the end of the world at all." Those passages are about the destruction of Jerusalem and "the end of the age of Israel."[34] The postmillennialist argues that this passage is pointing to the events that took place in AD 70. It would be difficult to argue that the list of terror in Matthew 24 more easily applies to our time than the time of Nero and Titus, and if Matthew 24:12 is applied to some future time of terror, it must be reconciled with Matthew 24:7, which claims that in that time nations will be at war. When compared to history, now is a time in which wars are rare.[35]

Later in that chapter, in Matthew 24:34, Jesus says, "I tell you the truth, this generation will not pass from the scene until all these things take place." The "these things" that Jesus is reference are the events of Matthew 24:29: "Immediately after the anguish of those days, 'the sun will be darkened, the moon will give no light, the stars will fall from the sky, and the powers in the heavens will be shaken.'" Verse 29 is quoting Isaiah 13:10 and 34:4. There is de-creation language like that of Matthew 24:29 throughout the Old Testament, and every time it occurs it is referencing a military destruction of a city or nation. It is logical, then, to conclude Jesus' warnings about terrible events that would happen are prophies about the destruction of a city or nation, and that is not surprising because the conversation in Matthew 24:1 that instigated this teaching from Jesus concerned the temple. The context was: "As Jesus was leaving the Temple grounds, his disciples pointed out to him the various Temple buildings. But he responded, "Do you see all these buildings? I tell you the truth, they will be completely demolished. Not one stone will be left on top of another!" Jesus was not talking about the end of time. Jesus was prophesying the destruction of Jerusalem that would happen within in one generation, just as Jesus said in Matthew 24:34.

34. Wilson, *Heaven Misplaced*, 102.

35. Geraghty, "There are a Lot of Reasons," para. 9.

The church has a clear commission, given from God, who has "all authority in heaven and on earth," and it is not to decline until Jesus returns to rescue the few who remain (Matt 28:18). That statement about God having all authority implies Satan has been bound. That commission is to "go and make disciples of all nations, baptizing them in the name of the Father and of the Son and of the Holy Spirit, and teaching them to obey everything I have commanded you. And surely I am with you always, to the very end of the age" (Matt 28:19–20). During the time of this present interadvent age, Satan cannot prevent the gospel from succeeding in bringing souls globally to faith in Christ. He can persecute the church, he can tempt people to sin, but Satan cannot stop the gospel.

A SUMMARY OF ESCHATOLOGY

A theory of eschatology that is growing in popularity is amillennialism. Amillennialists believe the millennium spoken of in Revelation 20 is either a metaphorical description of the period between Jesus' first and second coming or a heavenly reign of Christians who have died and are in an intermediate state, reigning until the second coming of Jesus. The differences between the moderate postmillennialist and amillennialist are nuanced, but they do separate significantly when the conversation of the future fate of the church begins. Kim Riddlebarger points out "many Postmillennial writers often describe the matter as a debate between 'optimistic' Postmillenarians and 'pessimistic' Amillenarians."[36]

The dispensationalist is the most eager to claim Christian suffering will continue and increase until the return of Jesus, but that belief is also held by most historical premillennialists (those who believe the second coming of Jesus will take place before the millennium but after the great tribulation) and amillennialists. In America, dispensationalism has far more adherence than amillennialism and postmillennialism combined.

Victory

The continued success of the church would inevitably lead to a decline in persecution. What was the victory Jesus Christ achieved when he was resurrected? The amillennialist sees the victory of Christ as primarily a

---

36. Riddlebarger, *Case for Amillennialism*, 96.

spiritual victory, but the postmillennialist argues the victory of Christ is in an ongoing physical reality. It is easy for the postmillennialists to come to an optimistic prediction for the church because they believe most of the prophecies about the end times that lead others to more morbid predictions have already been fulfilled.[37] In the same way Scripture describes the destruction of Jerusalem, the fall of empires, and the birth and death of kings in ways that "sound like Armageddon," radical imagery was used to talk about the end times, not in order to predict a literal fiery end to the space-time continuum, but because "radical imagery was the only language robust enough to sufficiently convey the magnitude of the spiritual, emotional, and historical situation."[38]

The Church of the Future

It is not surprising that a world so prone to pessimism has been attracted to a pessimistic eschatology. Clinging to a single guess about what will happen in the future, especially a guess that leads Christians to dread and an assumption of perpetual decline, may lead the church to self-fulfilling prophecy. In theory, dispensationalism has the same strategy for spreading the gospel to the whole world as the other theories of eschatology, but they do not believe they will succeed in their mission.

God will continue to bless his church as the church continues to seek ways to fulfill the Great Commission. Satan will not succeed in any of his attempts to thwart this mission. The church will overcome by the blood of the Lamb and the word of our testimony, with no desire to shrink from the call for fear of death (Rev 12:11). If the church does not succeed in its commission, Jesus was wrong, but we know that not even hell itself can stop that mission from succeeding. Jesus' credibility is at stake, but just as it has in the past, the church is now advancing all over the world.

DISCUSSION QUESTIONS:

   a. Have you decided which eschatological theory is most accurate? Why or why not?

---

37. Some of the passages postmillennialists use to back this optimistic view are Ps 2:6–9; 21:8–12; 110:12; Isa 2:24; 9:67; 11:6–10.

38. McNall, *Long Story Short*, 159.

b. Do you think there is value in talking about what will happen before, during, and after the second coming of Christ?

c. Why do you think the Bible doesn't clearly explain what will happen before, during, and after Jesus returns?

d. Second Timothy 3:19 talks about terrible times in the last days. Do you think that is a description of what the world was like in the past, what the world is like now, what the world will be like in the future, or all of the above?

7

Justification for Optimism

Christianity is on the rise worldwide, particularly in the Global South. Christianity also remains the world's largest faith, and the most distant projections to 2050 see it maintaining that lead.[1]

—BENJAMIN WORMALD

POTENTIAL FOR CHURCH GROWTH

PEOPLE DESIRE GROWTH. THEY want to grow personally even if they aren't willing to put in the work that growth will require, and people who desire personal growth want to associate themselves with growing organizations. They want to be part of a movement, not a tired club of rules. Christians have reason to be optimistic and even confident about the future growth of the Christian church, and America is primed for revival. Jesus referred to the imagery of a well-known phrase about crops being ready for harvest when he described people in need of eternal life as crops in need of harvesting (John 4:35–36). Jesus used this metaphor to motivate his followers to take action, to invite people to accept the gift of grace through faith. Like people in the first century, Americans are showing signs of being ripe for

1. Wormald, quoted in White, *Meet Generation Z*, 27.

98

harvest, but if Christians are going to become optimistic about the likelihood that the harvest is ready, they must understand how best to recognize and prepare for it.

Forework

Leonard Sweet says, "'Best practices' is working based on what you learned yesterday, but the half-life [the time it takes something to degenerate] of information is getting too short to rely completely on what has already happened."[2] The forward-thinking Christian will adopt semiotic practices that account for the past but act in accordance with what will happen in the future. This book will refer to the biblical practice of preparing for the future by reading the signs of the times with the past in mind as "forework."[3] In order to reach the youngest generations with the gospel, proper forework is necessary, and it appears the youngest generations are hungry for the discipleship this forework will provide.

A New Age

In an essay written just after the Second World War, historian Christopher Dawson explains there have been six identifiable "ages" in relation to the Christian church and faith, each lasting for three or four centuries and each following a similar course: each of these ages began and ended in crisis[4]: "The heart of each crisis was the same: intense attack by new enemies from within and from outside the church, which in turn demanded new spiritual determination and drive. Without this determination and drive, the church would have lost the day."[5] That is important! When crisis strikes, our temptation is to give up and assume we have lost, but the past can teach us that crisis is usually a sign that circumstances are about to improve. There has always been a number of determined Christians who fought through crisis, because they knew that without determination and drive, we would lose the day. The atrocities of World War II were a crisis that prepared the world for the greatest advancement of peace in history. The alliances and

2. Sweet, Lecture, Advance from Portland Seminary.

3. See Matt 16:23 and 1 Chr 12:32.

4. Dawson, "Six Ages of the Church," 34–45.

5. White, *Meet Generation Z*, 18.

agreements that resulted from the crisis propelled us forward. In his reflections on Dawson's essay, James Emery White says he believes "we are at the end of an age and stand at the beginning of another. A seventh age."[6] Like the beginning of a new school year for a seventh-grader, this new age brings excitement about a new period of growth and advancement, but it may also bring a voice change, growing pains, and acne.

Phyllis Tickle, like many historians, divides the past 2,000 years into 500-year cycles. She calls these cycles the "Greats:" The Great Transformation of the first century, the Great Decline of the sixth century, the Great Schism of the eleventh century, the Great Reformation of the sixteenth century, and now the Great Emergence of the twenty-first century. She claims the Great Emergence will be "equal in its impact" to the most impactful of the "Greats," the Great Transformation.[7] She agreed with the writings of Harvey Cox, who argued we are entering the third age of history that Joachim of Fiore called the Age of the Spirit.[8] Joachim developed a philosophy of history that contains three ages of increasing spirituality: the age of the Father, the Son, and the Holy Spirit.[9] Tickle and Cox believe we are entering the third age, the Age of the Spirit. Whether it is recognized as Pentecostalism, the Charismatic movement, Emergence Christianity, or the rise of the "spiritual but not religious," observers of Christianity recognize a shift has begun.[10] Proper forework that reflects this shift is now necessary.

If Tickle's theories about this 500-year cycle are true, we have much reason for excitement. Each of the periods have had three distinct results: a "new, more vital form of Christianity" emerges, a purer expression of Christianity arises, and, most importantly, "the faith has spread—and been spread—dramatically into new geographic and demographic areas, thereby increasing exponentially the range and depth of Christianity's reach as a result of its time of unease and distress."[11] In these times, the power centers of Christianity lose their power, and new growth results. The exponential growth is aided by the resulting split, which leaves the original system intact, although in a new form, while an entirely new system is created.

---

6. White, *Meet Generation Z*, 18.

7. Tickle, *Age of the Spirit*, 12.

8. Tickle, *Age of the Spirit*, 118.

9. Reeves, "Joachim of Fiore," para. 4.

10. Tickle, *Age of the Spirit*, 70.

11. Tickle and Shroyer, *Great Emergence*, 17.

The changes of these 500-year cycles aren't only being felt in the church. The world, as in past cycles, is experiencing unprecedented times of reconfiguration. Doug Sosnik writes America is "going through the most significant period of change since the beginning of the Industrial Revolution . . . Years from now we are going to look back at this period of time and see it as a 'hinge' moment . . . a connection point that ties two historical periods in time."[12] The world is seeing an increase in the number of people who consider themselves introverts,[13] a rise in depression,[14] and a widespread addiction to social media.[15] Those who pay attention to the happenings of the world have become increasingly aware the world is passing through almost unprecedented times of change.[16] James Emery White points out that

> identifying these "hinge moments" is actually a deeply biblical idea. The Bible lauds the men of Issachar for being sensitive to exactly these kinds of dynamics: "From the tribes of Issachar, there were 200 leaders . . . All these men understood the signs of the times and knew the best course for Israel to take" (1 Corinthians 12:32 NLT) . . . That tandem—knowing the signs of the times and how best to live in light of them—is key.[17]

If we are on the verge of a new age of Christianity, it is more important than ever to understand the semiotics of tomorrow and prioritize forework. If Christians want the church to flourish, they would be wise to understand the changes taking place. Otherwise, they face the potential of becoming irrelevant and time-bound, circling wagons with dreams of yesteryear. Dr. Leonard Sweet says, "if you want to hit a moving target, throw where the receiver is not."[18] Throw where the receiver is going to be.

12. Sosnik, "America's Hinge Moment," para. 6.

13. Guest, "How Digital Technology," para. 1.

14. Curran and Hill, "Perfectionism is Increasing," 420.

15. Bromwich, "Generation X More Addicted," para. 3.

16. Tickle, *Age of the Spirit*, 9.

17. White, *Meet Generation Z*, 18.

18. Sweet, Lecture, Advance from Portland Seminary.

Six Living Generations

Forework is necessary to prepare the church to shift into a culture with many generations. With the addition of Generation Z, there are six generations alive today, and a seventh is being born. As the life expectancy of people continues to rise, the number of generations alive at any given time will only increase. That is important to note, because "left to itself the church will grow old."[19] A generation does not naturally effectively evangelize the next generation. Compound this problem by six generations, and you have a major problem without a balancing effort to make "change" a core value. "If the natural flow of the church is to skew older, the leadership of the church must invest a disproportionate amount of energy and intentionality in order to maintain a vibrant population of young adults."[20] The necessary forework in a church that doesn't want to grow old will include employing and empowering young people, giving them responsibility early and often, prioritizing children and youth ministry, cultivating a culture of discipleship, etc. The church won't die with the death of older generations, but it will be healthier in the future if the older generations foster relationships with younger generations to pave the way for a healthy transfer of wisdom.

The good news is many of the church's sacred cows are dying. Rather than spending large amounts of money on hardwood pews, stained-glass windows, extravagant organs, and towering steeples, the church is spending money on child facilities. Rather than building large glass cathedrals, we are converting warehouses and old Kmarts into churches. Music styles have begun to evolve more quickly, and religious politics and unnecessary traditions are taking a back seat to community involvement. The methods of the church are changing, and changes are happening more easily.

REASON FOR OPTIMISM

Each age of Christianity begins and ends with frightening signs of decline, but the discouraging beginnings of each age are eclipsed by revivals, growth, and progress. It may seem the future of humanity looks grim, but open-minded historians would paint a more optimistic picture of the future.[21] Dr. Martin Luther King Jr. famously said " . . . the arc of the moral universe

---

19. White, *Meet Generation Z*, 147.

20. White, *Meet Generation Z*, 147.

21. Phipps, "Progress or Pessimism," para. 5.

is long but it bends toward justice."[22] The seventh-age theory provides a logical explanation that reconciles church decline statistics with the following proofs the church is not dying. First, Christianity is still growing, but the second and more convincing proof for Christians is a prophecy of Jesus Christ. Referring to the fact that Peter knew Jesus is the Son of the Living God, Jesus says to Peter, "Now I say to you that you are Peter (which means 'rock'), and upon this rock I will build my church, and all the powers of hell will not conquer it" (Matt 16:18 NLT).

Paving the Way for Pessimism

The reasons for optimism listed above have not convinced all Christian thinkers to adopt strategies that are driven by biblical optimism, including long-game forework. Winning the long game, as outlined by Steven Krupp and Paul Shoemaker, requires forework similar to the strategic plan of the War Conference to infiltrate Hollywood to make the world think more positively about the gay community,[23] Laurence Golborne to build a drill to rescue thirty-three miners trapped thousands of feet below ground,[24] and Nelson Mandela to lead a country at the brink of civil war toward peace and new prosperity.[25] With an optimistic long-game strategy, forward-thinking leaders were able to accomplish what seemed impossible when the pessimism of others limited their minds to short-game strategies. They believed in their ability to accomplish their goals, so they were persistent to carry out the forework that would do in the long-term what could not be accomplished in a short time.

The pessimism of the American Christian church has caused failure in implementing this principle, and their short-mindedness has contributed to the exodus of countless young people from the church.[26] Like most prominent American premillennialists, Dr. Adoniram Judson (A. J.) Gordon, who expected the papacy to produce the antichrist, "founded institutions and conducted ministerial affairs out of a theology of haste, not out

---

22. King, "Sermon at Temple Israel of Hollywood," para. 28.

23. War Conference, "Final Statement," para. 7.

24. Soto, "Chile to Dig Escape Shaft," para. 1.

25. Krupp and Shoemaker, *Winning the Long Game*, 209.

26. For evidence of the popularity of dispensationalism in America, see "Premillennialsm Reigns in Evangelical Theology," para. 5.

of a long-range vision for the health of Evangelical Christianity."[27] Scott M. Gibson reports American premillennialists stood against the postmillennialists' mission philosophy and strategy of a gradual conversion and universal righteousness on Earth. In fact, "the premillennialist did not guarantee or even expect the conversion of the world."[28] While they did demand the presentation of the gospel to everyone, they, like Jonah to the Ninevites, considered the preaching of the gospel as a "necessary preparation for the Second Coming of Christ's return."[29] The preaching of the gospel was done with a pessimistic doubt of widespread conversions. Although in the lifetime of A. J. Gordon (1836–1895) postmillennialism would continue to dominate North American theology, he and other theologians of his time sparked a shift in theological thought and practice. Rather than optimistically believe, like the postmillennialists, the world is bettering itself, that "war, famine, oppression, and slavery would be wiped out," premillennialists ridiculed the notion that the world would be converted to Christ.[30] Guided by Matthew 24:14, their focus shifted from the goal of conversion to the simpler goal of witness. Gordon asserts,

> Now to witness to the world and to win the world are not necessarily coextensive undertakings; and when the church shall have testified the gospel of the grace of God among all nations, it may be that multitudes will yet remain disobedient to the heavenly message. Therefore, I boldly affirm that the church has nowhere assigned to it the achievement of converting the world in the dispensation.[31]

Gordon, together with other premillennialists such as D. L. Moody and Arthur T. Pierson, paved the way for twentieth-century theologians to fully abandon long-game missional strategies that would reach the next generations and beyond.

27. Gibson and Gordon, *American Premillennialist*, xxiv.

28. Gibson and Gordon, *American Premillennialist*, 80.

29. Gibson and Gordon, *American Premillennialist*, 80.

30. Hiscox, "Pre-Millennial Theology," 2.

31. Gordon, *Holy Spirit in Missions*, 14.

Young Men

Throughout my life, I have heard Christians lament the absence of men in church. A more recent lament is the disturbing exodus of young people from the church. I believe both can be largely attributed to the church's pessimistic theology. Douglas Wilson writes,

> If they are taught, boys will respond to a clear statement of the mission before the church. Boys are built for battle, and they must be trained up to it. But if we continue to teach the hopelessness of all our earthly endeavors, we must not be surprised when those among us who are built, created, for earthly endeavors, take their strength elsewhere. Why do boys not like to come to church, we wonder? The answer is that we chase them out with our insipid and impotent doctrine.[32]

No intelligent young man is energized by the prospects of fighting for an army that is destined to lose or for a goal that cannot be achieved. The pessimism of dispensationalism repelled young men, and the absence of those young men has compounded the problem.

Men think church is for little old ladies of both sexes (a reflection on the feminine nature of men who go to church). Because feminine men were easily offended, we bowed to their emotions and retreated to politeness and removed masculine language from the pulpit. For example, feminine humor is cheesy and emotional, and many men like it. That is fine. Masculine humor is dumb and blunt, and many women like it. That is fine too. Both types of humor have merit. Both types of humor should have a place in church, but for too long the church only made room for one.

Similar things can be said about most hymns and worship songs. When I turn on the radio, my three-year-old son can tell you if a song he has never heard before is a "Christian" song or not. On a regular basis Lincoln says, "Daddy, this is a church song." Without fully understanding how, he has recognized that Christian songs have higher melodies, feminine politeness, soft/breathy vocalization, simple chords, and more sustained notes. Eventually, when he can understand just how over-spiritualized and mushy our language is, one of two things will happen: He will discover femininity within himself that was not there before, or he will rebel against the Christian norm. Instead of singing about fighting battles with God and his army, we sing about walking with him alone in gardens. The church

32. Wilson, *Future Men*, 51.

adopted theologies that teach us that we will lose the mission to win the world for Christ, so we focus our worship on surrender rather than momentum. It is good to surrender to God, not to surrender with God. The good news is that this error is reversible.

DISCUSSION QUESTIONS:

a. Is it good we have moved from building cathedrals and impressive stone buildings to converting warehouses and storefronts into churches?

b. Reflecting on Matthew 16:18, do you think Christians have good reason to be optimistic about the future?

c. What do you think the church of the future should look like?

d. Is there a role that you can play in discipling/leading the next generations?

8

The Youngest Generations

Discipleship is a bridge between generations.[1]

—GRANT SKELDON

AS THE TWENTYFIRST CENTURY becomes increasingly shortminded, instead of preparing for the future and adjusting accordingly, the modern American evangelical church chooses to criticize millennials rather than learn how to converse with them. Grant Skeldon, a millennial author, writes, "The one way to guarantee you will never understand us is to criticize us without spending time with us."[2] The impact of criticizing rather than conversing has taken a toll on the church, but, even worse than that, it caused the church to be completely blindsided by Generation Z, and Generation Z now constitutes 25.9 percent of the U.S. population.[3]

As we look at the characteristics of the generations of the future, we will see signs of eagerness to become part of a mission that gives meaning and purpose. This chapter will highlight their desire for optimistic mentors and hospitable fellowship, and it will explore the youngest generations alive in order to begin the forework necessary to reach future generations.

1. Skeldon, *Passion Generation*, 20.
2. Skeldon, *Passion Generation*, 23.
3. White, *Meet Generation Z*, 37.

THE IMAGE PROBLEM AND GENERATION Z

Christian leadership gurus have continued to focus on how to produce change in the next generation, talking about "the problem with millennials,"[4] but even the focus of their pessimism reveals their shortmindedness. The millennial generation is not the youngest generation. That title has long belonged to Generation Z (Gen Z) and is now being taken by another generation, yet to be named. There is a lot about the current form of the American evangelical church that clashes with Generation Z, and that generation now encompasses a quarter of our population and a far greater portion of those individuals who would be considered the "nones" or "outsiders." "The pattern is indisputable: The younger the generation, the more post-Christian it is."[5]

The church's swagger does not reflect the servant leadership and hospitable grace of the God Christians say they follow, and to the youngest generations, this disconnect is seen as hypocrisy.[6] The battle cry of many of the loudest Christians has focused more on the things about pre-Christians that annoy Christians rather than on love for the lost. This causes Christians to be seen as primarily judgmental and hypocritical, and the youngest generations feel rejected by Christians because they are being judged for behaviors that are prohibited by the Bible and even for behaviors that are not. Those people who claim to represent the love of Jesus have demonized sinners rather than shown them Christlike hospitality. This is why Christians are primarily seen as antihomosexual, judgmental, and hypocritical.

Is their opinion of Christians accurate? Partially, yes. All Christians believe they want people to be saved on a large scale, but many forget the people they say they want to reach make up the culture they attack so viciously. In addition, the pessimism dispensationalism has encouraged causes most Christians to believe most people will reject the gospel. When culture is seen as the enemy, judgmentalism results. Dr. Ryan Lokkesmoe suggests

> [t]here is an incongruity here that hinders our ability to find our friends in the community the way that Paul seemed to. On the one hand, we have a genuine love and concern for those who are unconnected to the church . . . And yet, many of us simultaneously

4. Khokunthod, "Problem with Millennials," para. 1.
5. Kinnaman, "Five Trends among the Unchurched," para. 7.
6. Kinnaman and Lyons, *Unchristian,* 342.

embrace a culture-war mentality toward those same people as a group. We feel threatened by "the culture" and the way we feel it is attacking Christian values. It seems we have forgotten that this monolithic, impersonal "culture" is made up of the same individuals we care so much about and design our ministries to reach. It's a tragic and debilitating contradiction.[7]

Perhaps this is why the Christian church in America is experiencing a reproduction crisis.

By looking at the characteristics of millennials and Generation Z, the rest of this chapter will reveal reasons for biblical optimism. If positivity will lead to success, the church can learn a lesson from Generation Z, which is currently the most optimistic generation alive.[8]

Founders

When MTV conducted a nationwide survey of 1,000 respondents born after the year 2000 to see how they would identify themselves if they had the choice, they came up with the self-important name "The Founders"—as in needing to "found the new world," rescuing it from the sins of the past.[9] Social entrepreneurship is one of Generation Z's most popular career choices.[10] Because they are the first generation to have a majority of members who believe the world is headed in the wrong direction, members of Gen Z have a strong sense of independence and an entrepreneurial spirit, attempting to take things into their own hands to correct the mistakes of the previous generations, and that is from where their optimism comes. Partially due to the near disappearance of extreme poverty, they believe they can do it. Gen Z will not accept the conclusions of previous generations without at least reimagining them.

Logan LaPlante, a member of Generation Z, calls the best members of his generation "Hackers." He says "Hackers are innovators. Hackers are people who challenge and change the system to make them work differently. To make them work better . . . I'm growing up in a world that needs more people with a hacker mindset."[11] Robert Noyce, co-founder of Intel,

7. Lokkesmoe, *Paul and His Team*, 113.

8. Kalish, "Millennials are the Least Wealthy."

9. White, *Meet Generation Z*, 433

10. Lesonsky, "Rise of Gen Z Entrepreneurs," para. 5.

11. LaPlante, "Hackschooling Makes Me Happy," 5:22–5:37.

once said optimism is "an essential ingredient of innovation. How else can the individual welcome change over security, adventure over staying in safe places?"[12] According to Carmine Gallo, optimists are the best entrepreneurs, largely because they are inspiring communicators who rally people to a better future. The founders of the youngest generations will be drawn to an optimistic church.[13]

Digital Connection

Research from the Wharton School declares that "already one defining characteristic is abundantly clear: This generation is Wi-Fi enabled."[14] They have a comfort level with technology that dwarfs that of previous generations. David Bell calls them the "Internet-in-its-pocket" generation.[15] Teenagers spend nearly nine hours a day absorbing media.[16] As James Emery White comments, "The implications of this constant connection to the internet and, through it, the world and all of its information leads to . . . the 'ability to find whatever they're after without the help of intermediaries—such as libraries, shops, or teachers.' This has made them 'more independent and self-directed than the generation before them.'"[17] What then do they need the church for? What do they need pastors for? What is the church offering these young people that they can't get online? The data is easily accessible, but trusted interpreters are needed. They need teachers and pastors who will interpret the data in light of Jesus and his kingdom. It won't work to simply criticize the Kardashians. The church must interpret the Kardashians in some meaningful way. Has the church prioritized things that will keep Gen Z connected to it, such as community and fellowship, opportunities to serve, emotionally impactful environments, mentorship, etc.? The successful church will. If the church continues to become more cynical and judgmental, it will not. If we want to know what the church should focus on in the future, we should ask ourselves, "What does the church provide for people that podcasts don't?"

12. Gallo, "5 Reasons Why," para. 1.
13. Gallo, "5 Reasons Why," para. 1.
14. "'Millennials on Steroids,'" para. 4.
15. "'Millennials on Steroids,'" para. 4.
16. Lien, "Teens Spend an Average of 9 Hours a Day," para. 1.
17. White, *Meet Generation Z*, 44.

It should be a source of great optimism for the church that Generation Z recognizes the flaw in the millennial preference for online interaction (a fact that is changing), and only 15 percent of Gen Z prefers to interact with their friends via social media rather than face to face.[18] In fact, even when they do interact online, they have adopted face-to-face options like Face-Time like no generation before.[19] They have begun to reverse the trend of physical disconnectedness.[20] This could be a wide-open door for the church to step in and connect with this generation in a way that education and entertainment will not.

Seeking Wisdom

Seventy-eighty percent of Gen Z still believes in the existence of God, but only 41 percent attend weekly religious services, and only 8 percent would cite a religious leader as a role model. So, who are their role models? No one knows, not even them. They are still searching for them. In fact, a staggering 75 percent of the members of Gen Z are looking for a mentor.[21] Unlike previous generations, their parents failed to serve as positive role models.

> One of the marks of Generation Z is that they are being raised, by and large, by Generation X—a generation that was warned repeatedly not to become "helicopter" parents (i.e., always hovering over their children). As a result, Generation Z has been given more space and more independence than any other generation. This means that Generation Z is very self-directed.[22]

They are "leaderless."[23] Their families have, on average, done little to direct them or hand them a narrative of life that works. This has resulted in a generation that has knowledge beyond any generation before, but they lack the ability to interpret that knowledge. They are desperate for the wisdom mentors would provide. This would explain ISIS's success in recruiting young people.[24] The youngest generations "have access to more

---

18. Lenhart et al., "Teens, Technology and Romantic Relationships," 7.
19. White, *Meet Generation Z*, 45.
20. Jenkins, "15 Aspects," para. 4.
21. Shore, "Turning on the 'No-Collar' Workforce," para. 12.
22. White, *Meet Generation Z*, 51.
23. White, *Meet Generation Z*, 65.
24. White, *Meet Generation Z*, 126.

knowledge content than any other generation in human history, but many lack discernment for how to wisely apply that knowledge to their lives and world."[25]

Young people are searching for wisdom. "Within our world, there is an amazingly deep sense of awe and wonder about the universe. And the ones who [feel] this the most" is Generation Z.[26] ISIS stole some of our best metaphors and used them to attract thousands to an evil cause, however, they are not the first generation to come to horrible conclusions in a search for truth and meaning. The German notion of the Führer came from a generation searching for meaning and "guidance out of its troubles."[27] They are searching for confident, optimistic leaders who believe they can change the world.

In order to reach Gen Z, proper forework will involve engagement with their questions, viewpoints, and perspectives. Christians should enter into their chat rooms, respond to their blogs, and answer their tweets with grace and relevance. ISIS maintained 24-hour online operation, and before military efforts thwarted many of their efforts, their effectiveness was expanded by larger rings of sympathetic volunteers and fans who passed on its messages and viewpoints, reeling in potential recruits.[28] They successfully turned their followers into evangelists. How much more can Christians accomplish with a message of hope? George Washington wrote, "Truth will ultimately prevail where pains is taken to bring it to light."[29] Truth is a powerful force that makes a great ally in just pursuits (John 8:32).

Evangelists

On June 11, 2007, Apple published a press release that would forever change our world. It was titled "iPhone to Support Third-Party Web 2.0 Applications."[30] Apple inspired and empowered their followers to be their evangelists. They did it by giving their followers the power to create, to found new technologies, to launch apps. As Founders, the members of Gen

---

25. Kinnaman, *You Lost Me*, 30.

26. White, *Meet Generation Z*, 136.

27. Mataxas, *Bonhoeffer*, 141.

28. White, *Meet Generation Z*, 126.

29. National Archives, "From George Washington to Charles Mynn Thruston," para. 4.

30. Apple, "iPhone to Support," para. 1.

Z are evangelists of their favorite brands, politicians, and celebrities. A hospitable, gracious, and benevolent church could tap into this potential more than a piece of technology could. Their energy could bring excitement to the church for the potential of tangible life change in our world on a revolutionary scale. In *The Gospel According to Starbucks*, Leonard Sweet writes, "Jesus recommended that his disciples learn something from the wisdom of the world. He observed that 'the people of this world' pursue their dreams with greater passion and intelligence than 'the people of the light.'"[31] The church may have to educate itself in the ways of Apple in order to again become creators of dream fulfillment rather than fighters of unnecessary battles.

In *Nudge*, Leonard Sweet suggests, "for the twenty-first century, evangelism will be built on nudges that have more to do with life before death than death and the afterlife, that focus more on the love of Christ than the wrath of God, that worry less about dying than about never having lived."[32] That would be an optimistic movement Generation Z would love to evangelize for, and that is a life they want to live. Our lives are stories, but Boomers are planners who want to take the best-case scenario and turn it into a strategic plan. The future is coming at us too fast for that, and it is full of surprises. That is one reason churches are getting hit so hard. Due to a lack of forework, Christians weren't ready for the future with the right metaphors or the right tone. The most practical thing a person can come up with to guide him or her into the future is a metaphor and a nudge toward life and love.

Like secular social marketing organizations, the church can create little ambassadors who will evangelize the world. How could Christians do this? By being the best storytellers. The effectiveness of a sales tactic has a relatively short lifespan, but the really good stories are eternally effective recruiters. Jesus spent most of his ministry teaching his followers to be confident, optimistic storytellers, but Christians attempt to systematize the stories and make them linear. They see the stories as a tool to create systematic theology rather than as the theology itself. By calling the story of Jesus a theography, Leonard Sweet argues the story of God is theology.[33] If Christians could perfect the art of telling stories, they could do more to make disciples of all nations.

31. Sweet, *Gospel According to Starbucks*, 5.

32. Sweet, *Nudge*, 32.

33. Sweet and Viola, *Jesus*, ix.

Geoff White, the North America Digital Brand Manager for Nike Women and Men's Training, says Nike "can't sell products that don't have a good story."[34] Today's marketers have recognized that the successful campaign will tell true brand stories, get more personal, realize less is more, and get to the point.[35] In a personal interview on June 17, 2016, he explained, "It's not about pushing product on people. It's about making Nike part of a story."[36] This story-centricity and an increase in visual communication technologies (emoji, FaceTime, Skype, etc.), have led Generation Z to be the most visual generation in history.[37]

Seeking Authenticity

Like millennials, Generation Z is on a mission to seek out that which is authentic.[38] Geoff White says it's no longer helpful to advertise products in fictional scenarios. Millennials and Gen Z want to know there is a heart behind the story of the products for which they choose to become evangelists. He goes on to say, "We hire the best Instagram photographers to photograph authentic sport in its natural habitat, and we place Nike in that story. We don't just show the product. We show our product being used in an authentic space. Young people don't want to see Kobe Bryant playing basketball in an arena. They want to see him working out behind the scenes."[39]

Ken Tennyson recognized a dynamic at work in the youngest generations when he said,

> Reality television is often bemoaned for its lack of meaningful content and its voyeuristic tendencies . . . I am interested in why it is so popular given the oft expressed discontent. An unscripted, live shooting represents an actual event, a one-time occurrence that shows its imperfections as well as triumphs . . . Instead of a clean, linear story that has a clear ending, reality T.V. tells many stories simultaneously, and the ending is often messy and unfinished . . .

34. White, personal interview, June 17, 2016.
35. Daykin, "Five Things Great Brands Will Do," paras. 3–5.
36. White, personal interview, June 17, 2016.
37. White, *Meet Generation Z*, 117.
38. Pew Research Center, "Millennials in Adulthood," para. 7.
39. White, personal interview, June 17, 2016.

It seems to me that a hunger for authenticity and adventure drive the current trend in reality T.V.[40]

The successful church of the future will be authentic, which means a departure from the current pedestrian church to a participatory church model.[41]

Participatory

Many have argued podcasts and online church will overtake the current form of church. If there is one thing COVID-19 has taught me, it's that online church will not replace in-person church. Online church can serve as a helpful tool, but it is not a replacement. It doesn't work for relationship development, mentorship, discipleship, corporate worship, etc. The development of the voice of the individual also suggests people desire to have a voice or personally know the voice they listen to (blogs, likes, comments, etc.). The satellite church will need to accommodate this paradigm shift if it is to have longevity.[42] Leonard Sweet calls these young generations a Karaoke Culture.[43] People want their voice to be heard.

The younger generations have introduced a shift in the way people socialize and build relationships. This change is evident in social media platforms and coffee shops. In a CBS interview, Katie Couric asked Howard Shultz, the CEO of Starbucks, "When you look around a Starbucks, what do you see?" His response explains why Starbucks has so successfully met the needs of this social generation. "I see a deep sense of community," he replied. "We've intended, from day one, to really kind of build a third place between home and work. And really, I think at a time in America where people are hungry for human connection, we're providing that."[44] Starbucks is currently fulfilling the need for a third place. The church is perfectly positioned to step back into that role. The church can become known as the friendliest place in America. Why are Christians looking to Starbucks for insight on creating an environment conducive to relationship-building when the God-man we follow was the greatest social marketer in history?

40. Tennyson, "Semiotic Awareness," para. 9.

41. Sweeney, "Leonard Sweet on Signs," para. 8.

42. Tennyson, "Semiotic Awareness."

43. Sweet, *Nudge*.

44. CBS News, "Starbucks CEO Howard Schultz is All Abuzz," para. 3.

And the product Christians offer is free, graceful, and available to all. This social evolution represents the greatest opportunity for church growth.

This reveals another error in the way the Christian evangelistic strategy has failed. Leonard Sweet writes,

> Christians have much to learn about faith as a lived experience, not a thought experiment. Rational faith—the form of Christianity that relies on argument, logic, and apologetics to establish and defend its rightness—has failed miserably in meeting people where they live. Intellectual arguments over doctrine and theology are fine for divinity school, but they lose impact at the level of daily life experience. Starbucks knows that people live for engagement, connection, symbols, and meaningful experiences. If you read the Bible, you'll see that the people of God throughout history have known the same thing. Life at its very best is a passionate experience, not a doctoral dissertation.[45]

Later, he adds, "Today, too many Christians line up to follow God out of duty or guilt, or even hoping to win a ticket to heaven. They completely miss the warmth and richness of the experience of living with God. They fail to pick up the aroma of what God is doing in their part of town."[46] That warmth and richness would be very attractive to Generation Z.

One of the primary changes that needs to occur in the church is a shift from rows of people judging a preacher's theology and style to authentic, participatory circles of people discussing strategies and ideas that will touch the hearts of young people. Ben Reed, author of *Starting Small*, says, "If you are really committed to spiritual formation, you've got to have a system that allows everybody to participate."[47] Circles are much more conducive to the Gen Z priorities of fellowship, mentorship, service, and emotional support. In circles, where two-way communication is valued, hospitality comes more naturally, and relational care is superior to pastoral care.[48] These are the qualities of a church that can reach the youngest generations.

The signs of ripeness are undeniable. The potential for growth is great. As the church shifts from assumed mission failure to optimistic hope for the future, it will realize the benefits that positivity can have on a group of people. In order to reach new people rather than rely on addition solely by

---

45. Sweet, *Gospel According to Starbucks*, 5.
46. Sweet, *Gospel According to Starbucks*, 5.
47. Reed, "Why Circles are Better than Rows," para. 7.
48. Reed, "Why Circles are Better than Rows," para. 9.

handing our faith to our offspring (something else we aren't good at), the church will need to utilize the attractive and motivating qualities of positive networkers and authentic community.

Spiritually Illiterate

The church is not losing millennials and Generation Z because they have weighed the claims of Christianity and found them to be unacceptable. They are leaving the church because they are ignorant of the claims of Christianity. They don't engage with Christian ideas because they don't see a need for the church. In other words, they are resistant to Christians, not to Christ.

James Emery White says, "Perhaps the most defining mark of members of Generation Z, in terms of their spiritual lives, is their spiritual illiteracy . . . They do not know what the Bible says . . . They are more than post-Christian. They don't even have a memory of the gospel."[49] Part of this shift is due to Generation Z's feeling that they don't need to have spiritual or religious knowledge because of the vast amount of information so readily available on their devices. Due to this paradigm, Chuck Kelley, president of New Orleans Baptist Theological Seminary, points out the new task of education is to "help students evaluate information."[50] Young people had access to information about ISIS, but they were unable to evaluate the value and reliability of the information.

In *Good Faith*, David Kinnaman and Gabe Lyons say that "growing numbers of adults, and especially younger adults, have no inkling that Christianity matters and could matter to them. Furthermore, they have little appreciation for how Christians generate good in the world."[51] There is now an opportunity to introduce a new kind of Christianity that actually reflects the intentions of Christ.

Meaning and the Future

A reason for optimism about the future is that spirituality is important to young adults. The thirst for God is still there. "How could it not be," says

49. White, *Meet Generation Z*, 131.

50. Myers, "Theological Ed. is 'Being Redefined,'" para. 11.

51. Kinnaman and Lyons, *Good Faith*, 21.

Thom Schultz, "when the profoundest human questions—Why does the universe exist rather than nothing? How did humanity come to be on this remote blue speck of a planet? What happens to us after death?—remain as pressing and mysterious as they've always been?"[52] Later in his writing, he expounds on this idea when he says, "Consider these encouraging statistics: 91 percent say they believe in God. 88 percent say faith is important."[53] The polls show a huge majority of Americans still believe in a higher power, but the challenge enters the equation when we recognize most young adults consider spirituality just one element of a successful, eclectic life. "Fewer than one out of ten young adults mention faith as their top priority."[54]

After living a life of wealth and plenty, Matthew recognized the things of this world will fade away. He quotes Jesus, saying, "Do not store up for yourselves treasures on earth, where moths and vermin destroy, and where thieves break in and steal. But store up for yourselves treasures in heaven, where moths and vermin do not destroy, and where thieves do not break in and steal" (Matt 6:19–20). When the world attempts to offer meaning, it inevitably offers a perishing good that will soon disappoint its recipient. One of the elementary principles of the Christian faith is that only God offers lasting meaning. Here's what Shawn Achor says about meaning:

> If the mental map you are using lacks meaning markers, it is incomplete and inaccurate and can lead you astray. Meaning markers are quite simply those things in your life that matter to you: career advancement, a new business, your kid's admission to a desired school, better health, your faith, and so on. No matter what goal or challenge you set for yourself, if you want to be able to channel your full range of intelligences toward achieving it, your personal meaning markers should be points on your mental path. So, if you're currently finding your work less meaningful, your obstacles less surmountable, or your goals less attainable, chances are you need to redraw your mental map. Truth be told, we could all really use help finding more meaning in our lives. In *The Happiness Advantage*, I defined happiness as "the joy we feel moving toward our potential." A lack of meaning in our reality robs us not only of that joy, but also our ability to use our multiple intelligences to

---

52. Schultz, *Why Nobody Wants*, 215.

53. Schultz, *Why Nobody Wants*, 482.

54. Kinnaman and Lyons, *Unchristian*, 293.

increase our success, but as we have seen, a high IQ or EQ alone won't help us find meaning along our paths.[55]

The Christian faith has the "help" Achor is looking for, and that will never change. This should be a source of logical optimism for the Christian church.

CHANGE

It seems harsh to say, but the church has long relied on the death of the oldest generations for change. On the surface, it revealed itself through battles like the worship wars that were fueled by the growing range of style preferences due to the growing number of generations represented in each church. Generation X loved their pews, but the millennials couldn't wait to replace them with chairs. Each generation puts its own twist on theologies, adopts unique communication styles, and develops its own structures.[56] With six generations currently alive, change is not happening fast enough for the church to do what is necessary to reach the youngest generations. Each generation has unique tendencies, struggles, and story-forming experiences. The church needs to learn the stories that will reach the next generations, and focus their methods on those stories. When the church is at its best, change and evolving methods are a core value rather than a natural result of lifecycles.

DISCUSSION QUESTIONS:

a. How do we keep from waging a culture war on the lost people we are called to lead to Christ? How do we look past their sinful behavior to see the depraved person in need of a spiritual doctor?

b. What is the difference between knowledge and wisdom? What is the danger of having such a large amount of knowledge without the wisdom and experience to understand how to apply that knowledge in constructive ways?

---

55. Achor, *Before Happiness*, 69.
56. O'Brian, "Christ, Culture, and the Generation Gap," para. 5.

c. Can you think of ways Christians can step into the mentoring role Generation Z is so desperate for? Is this an appropriate role for the church to play?

d. For generations, churches have fought younger generations over music, secondary theologies, traditions, apparel, etc. Change is necessary for growth, and things that don't change die. What can the church do to make "change" a core value and avoid clinging to unnecessary traditions?

9

A History of Positivity in the Church

If we believe in the final triumph of the kingdom, it follows that there will come a time when revivals will no longer be necessary. But while there is a single impenitent child of God, revivals in some form or other will be a necessity for bringing such into the fold of Christ.[1]

—FRANK BEARDLEY

CHRISTIANS MAKE CHRISTIANS. As we become who we were created to be, we learn to love people sacrificially, and that love leads us to introduce people to the One who makes our lives better and makes us better at life. We are drawn to Jesus for selfish reasons, but as we mature spiritually our love for him becomes sacrificial. That sacrificial love focuses its attention on sharing the love. This concept is also seen in the way the best relationships start with a romantic attraction, move to sacrificial love, then spread that love to offspring. Similarly, the body of Christ can't help but reproduce the faith by adopting other people into the family of God. In other words, when Christians grow, the church grows. In order to help Christians see that positivity aids this growth, this chapter will describe methods the church has used to thrive in the past. If we don't know why we were successful in the past, we won't be able to repeat that success, and in the past, positivity led to success. In order to gain a positive mindset, Christians who

1. Beardsley, *History of American Revivals,* loc. 3097 of 3153.

seek evidence for the potential of future thriving can take notes from the example set by many of the church's great leaders. This chapter will look at the church that was formed by these optimistic leaders and the ideas that made them the personalities who would attract so many to the Christian faith. Positivity will lead to church growth.

THE JOY OF REVIVAL

Christianity is in need of a joyful revival, and the power of revivals to bring people to Christ is connected to its ability to produce joy. In *The Treasury of David*, Charles Spurgeon writes, "A genuine revival without joy in the Lord is as impossible as spring without flowers."[2] Psalm 85:6 says, "Will you not revive us again, that your people may rejoice in you?" Church growth leads to rejoicing, and the emotion associated with the action of rejoicing is joy. Joy is intricately connected to church growth. Throughout the history of Christianity, revival has served as a bringer of joy and therefore the benefits of positivity. Revivals produce the fruit of the Spirit, not the least of which is joy.

Revival, Reformation, and Awakening

Jeremiah Johnson suggests individual evangelism may not be enough. In fact, he says, "revival" might not be the right word because it implies something short-term. That has led him to use the word "reformation." He says, "The church has settled for a small vision; maybe a much smaller one than God would have intended."[3] When I use the word "revival," I intend it to imply the large-scale, long-term transformation and growth of the Christian church.

In a fair statement made about the limits of the word "revival," Greg Laurie points out that "[a]n awakening takes place when God sovereignly pours out his Spirit and it impacts a culture . . . A revival, on the other hand, is what the church must experience. It's when the church comes back to life, when the church becomes what it was always meant to be."[4] His point is the word "revival" generally focuses on the rejuvenation of Christians,

---

2. Spurgeon, *Treasury of David*, 86.

3. Strand, "Time for a Second Reformation?," para. 10.

4. Laurie, "What is the Difference?," para. 4.

and the word "awakening" generally focuses on pre-Christians becoming Christians. This is a true observation, but because of the inseparable connection of evangelism and discipleship, like fruit to a grafted branch, I will periodically use the words "revival" and "awakening" interchangeably. Gordon MacDonald says hope sparks revival, and revivals produce followers of Christ.[5] The people God used to lead the great Christian revivals demonstrated the effects that hope, joy, and positivity can have on producing revivals and Christian advancement. The following is an examination of some of those people.

JONATHAN EDWARDS AND CHURCH GROWTH

The eighteenth century brought many great changes to the world. It saw the rise of capitalism and the middle class, the Industrial Revolution, a depoliticizing of the Christian church, and arguably the greatest Christian revival in history. Paul Moore argues the Great Awakening and its sister revivals around the world produced "the greatest change in society in the history of modern man."[6] Its impact was not only felt in the church, but in all areas of life, and this happy period in history encouraged Christians to adopt positivity and optimistic theologies. Or was it the other way around? In reflecting on this great revival, Jonathan Edwards, an eighteenth-century revivalist, preacher, philosopher, and theologian, says,

> We are taught also by this happy event how easy it will be for our blessed Lord to make a full accomplishment of all his predictions concerning his kingdom, and to spread his dominion from sea to sea, thro' all the nations of the earth. We see how easy it is for him with one turn of his hand, with one word of his mouth, to awaken whole countries of stupid and sleeping sinners, and kindle divine life in their souls.[7]

It was this incredible optimism concerning God's plan for this world that led Edwards to write sermons that would spread the gospel of grace through faith throughout our world and challenge "the old forms of religious authority."[8] That optimism and courage were motived by some key

5. MacDonald, "Beyond Pessimism or Pessimism," para. 7.

6. Moore, *Revival*, 745.

7. Edwards, *Jonathan Edwards*, 5.

8. Koester, *Introduction to the History of Christianity*, 38.

points of his theology.[9] Two of those beliefs were justification by faith alone and postmillennialism. Although he was most known for his revival sermon, "Sinners in the Hands of an Angry God," he spent "much less time and energy depicting the wrath of God than he did preparing sermons about the beauties of Christ's perfections."[10] About this sermon, Dr. Dane C. Ortlund writes, "The hellfire sermons were more typical of the young Edwards and gradually decreased over his career, while other themes grew increasingly strong: the beauty of Christ, the loveliness of holiness, the calmness of a justified life, the gentleness of God."[11]

By Grace through Faith

As shown in previous chapters, the image problem of the church is largely caused by the church's judgment of the actions of pre-Christians. If it were actions that saved people from the eternal consequence of sinful actions, that judgmentalism might be justified, but it is not the actions of Christians that save them—it is the actions of Jesus Christ. The passage Edwards quoted most is John 1:12: "Yet to all who did receive him, to those who believed in his name, he gave the right to become children of God."[12] A hospitable and inclusive belief in God's grace led Edwards to an inclusive strategy of evangelism.

This grace-focused teaching is not unique to the Great Awakening. From Paul Moore's extensive study of the social conditions surrounding revivals, he concludes: "revival is a gift of grace—in spite of man's rebellion . . . When the law is powerless to bring about change, God invades the atmosphere and rescues men from their own depravity."[13]

Postmillennialism

Edwards's self-efficacy and optimistic evangelistic strategies are also seen in his eschatological beliefs. Edwards was a postmillennialist. Loraine Boettner, in the tradition of Athanasius, gives a description of postmillennialism that

9. Koester, *Introduction to the History of Christianity*, 39.

10. Noll, *History of Christianity*, 95.

11. Ortlund, "5 Things Jonathan Edwards Teaches Us," para. 19.

12. Edwards, *Jonathan Edwards*, 427.

13. Moore, *Revival*, loc. 1674 of 2112.

connects Edwards's actions to his eschatology, describing postmillennialism as the "view of the last things which holds that the kingdom of God
is now being extended in the world through the preaching of the Gospel
and the saving work of the Holy Spirit and that the world eventually will
be Christianized."[14] While dispensationalists, like Irenaeus, believe any effort to make this world a better place will only delay the second coming,
postmillennialists foster a spirit of excitement for the future of the mission
with which we participate.[15]

As "Yale's first and foremost child prodigy," Edwards clearly did not
lack biblical knowledge in coming to that belief. In fact, he was brilliant.

> Jonathan Edwards matriculated at Yale (then Collegiate School
> of Connecticut) in 1716 just before reaching 13. At the time,
> entrance into the college required fluency in Latin, Greek, and
> Hebrew. Four years and one intense conversion later, he gradu-
> ated as valedictorian, received his Masters of Divinity from Yale
> in 1722 and went on to become one of America's most renowned
> theologians and philosophers.[16]

In his research, Edwards became extremely interested in eschatological studies. He wrote a commentary on Revelation as he attempted to
determine the things that would come after life on this earth. He eventually understood that the prophecies in the Old Testament about the great
kingdom really referred to the church, as it became God's kingdom on the
earth.[17]

Jonathan Edwards begins his book, *A Humble Attempt*, with a prophecy from Zechariah 8:20–22 that points to a time when the nations would
come to Jerusalem to inquire of the Lord. He believed this would happen
during the church age when gentile nations would be converted to Christianity. Edwards writes, "In this chapter Zechariah prophesies of the future,
glorious advancement of the church. It is evident there is more intended
than was ever fulfilled in the Jewish nation during Old Testament times."[18]

Edwards felt he was seeing the beginning of a move of God that could
continue to the ends of the earth. In *A Humble Attempt*, Edwards points

---

14. Boettner, *Postmillenialism*, 72.

15. Garner, *Why the End is Not Near*, 816.

16. "History," para. 5.

17. Edwards, *Jonathan Edwards*, 529.

18. Edwards, *Humble Attempt to Promote Explicit Agreement*, 132.

out his strong belief that the nations of the world will gather in Jerusalem, seeking God. He emphasizes this by quoting Isaiah 60:24:

> See, darkness covers the earth and thick darkness is over the peoples, but the Lord rises upon you and his glory appears over you. Nations will come to your light, and kings to the brightness of your dawn. Lift up your eyes and look about you: All assemble and come to you; your sons come from afar, and your daughters are carried on the arm.

This is perhaps the most optimistic of all interpretations concerning the church, and it was held by one of the most intelligent gospel preachers in history. Jonathan Edwards believed the church is God's plan to succeed in discipling the world.

Thy Kingdom Come

Jesus taught his followers to pray, "Thy kingdom come, thy will be done on earth as it is in heaven" (Matt 6:10). Edwards confidently prayed this prayer, fully expecting God would use the church to actually usher in his reign over the earth, and Edwards determined to meet this state of mind by regularly including the imminence of the kingdom in his preaching. It is likely optimistic Christians will look forward to the new heaven and the new earth, but not in the way a child looks forward to the conclusion of a punishment (2 Pet 3:13). Instead they should work toward that day like a bride works in excitement to prepare for her wedding.

Similar to the way the old law prepared the world to understand the new law, this world prepares humans for the next world, but what will the next world look like? Heaven is not a completely separated existence that ignores the present world. It is an excellent evolution of this world. Randy Alcorn explains that on the new earth, Christians will say, "the reason we loved the old earth is that sometimes it looked a little like this."[19] He continues, "The bucket-list mentality reveals an impoverished view of redemption. Even Christians end up thinking, 'If I can't live my dreams now, I never will.'"

To conclude that the eternal destination of Christians is an ethereal place in the sky is a departure from the traditional understanding of heaven. Douglas Wilson points out "the Bible doesn't generally speak in our

---

19. Alcorn, "C.S. Lewis on Heaven and the New Earth," para. 112.

popular way of 'going to heaven when we die'—not that it is technically wrong . . . the final biblical hope is heaven coming here."[20] Christians pray to the sky when speaking to God, but that is because that is where Jesus went. It is also where he will come from when he returns to earth. The kingdom comes. It does not go.

Ed Love writes, "The pious escapist believes that the world is a wicked place and the primary hope of the Christian is that he or she can have the assurance of an otherworldly heaven."[21] On the topic of the church's image problem, Gabe Lyons points to the need for Christians to be the light of the world and the salt of the earth, not "sheltered" and "insulated" from the world.[22]

The Great Awakening

The optimism and confidence of Jonathan Edwards were contagious, and people began to join him in prayer for revival. Edwards was an intelligent and emotional leader with both depth and charisma. Edwards says, "The time will come when there will not be one nation remaining in the world, which shall not embrace the true religion."[23] His vision itself was attractive. He argued that Isaiah 60:12 demonstrates the nation that will not serve God will perish, and heathen idolatry will be destroyed, as shown in Jeremiah 10:11: "While this earth and these heavens remain." That is to say, it would happen before the end of the world.[24]

In Northampton one Sunday morning in 1734, the Great Awakening saw its beginning. It came suddenly; over a short period of time about 300 people came to know Christ as their Savior. Edwards describes the time in his book *Faithful Narrative of the Surprising Work of God*, "There was scarcely a single person in the town, old or young, left unconcerned about the great things of the eternal world." Edwards goes on to explain:

> Our public assemblies were then beautiful: the congregation was alive in God's service, every one earnestly intent on the public worship, every hearer eager to drink in the words of the minister as they came from his mouth; the assembly in general were, from

20. Wilson, *Heaven Misplaced*, 21.

21. Love, "Coming God," v.

22. Lyons, "Christianity Has an Image Problem," para. 25.

23. Edwards, Rogers, Dwight, and Hickman, *Works of Jonathan Edwards*, 286.

24. Edwards, *Humble Attempt to Promote Explicit Agreement*, 943.

time to time, in tears while the word was preached; some weeping with sorrow and distress, others with joy and love, others with pity and concern for the souls of their neighbors.[25]

It affected all sorts of people, "sober and vicious, high and low, rich and poor, wise and unwise."[26] No one was considered too far gone to be saved. Sinners were not rejected or criticized but offered extravagant hospitality.

A Sovereign Act of God

It could be argued revival and church growth are sovereign acts of God that cannot be instigated by human action, but Jonathan Edwards's belief in the sovereignty of God did not keep him from working for revival. Edwards was a reformed theologian who said, "He who would set the hearts of other men on fire with the love of Christ must himself burn with love."[27] His acknowledgment of man's ability to set the hearts of other men on fire shows he saw no conflict between God's sovereignty and man's initiating role. Pastors Shyju and Tiny Mathew believe revival is a sovereign act of God, but when God sparks revival he does so while "looking for an active and conscious pursuit of him."[28] Even those who believe in a very limited human role in the instigation of spiritual awakenings point to God's commands as reason for evangelism and discipleship.[29]

JOHN WESLEY

John Wesley never taught a specific eschatological theory as fact, but he worked as if he believed the world would be Christianized. It would be difficult to argue Wesley was not optimistic about the future of the church. In a sermon titled "The General Spread of the Gospel," Wesley quoted Isaiah 11:9, "They will neither harm nor destroy on all my holy mountain, for the earth will be filled with the knowledge of the Lord as the waters cover the sea," and Wesley added, "There will then, very probably, be a great shaking; but I cannot induce myself to think that God has wrought so glorious a

25. Edwards, "Faithful Narrative of the Surprising Work of God," 27.

26. Edwards, "Faithful Narrative of the Surprising Work of God," 31.

27. Murray, "Jonathan Edwards," para. 36.

28. Mathew and Mathew, "Why Does 'Revival?,'" para. 9.

29. Sproul, "Predestination and Evangelism," para. 3.

work, to let it sink and die away in a few years. No: I trust this is only the beginning of a far greater work; the dawn of 'the latter day glory.'"[30] In his sermon "The Signs of the Times," Wesley said,

> The times which we have reason to believe are at hand, (if they are not already begun) are what many pious men have termed, the time of 'the latter-day glory'—meaning the time wherein God would gloriously display his power and love, in the fulfillment of his gracious promise that 'the knowledge of the Lord shall cover the earth, as the waters cover the sea.'[31]

Wesley famously extended the work of salvation past justification to sanctification, believing followers of Christ can actually become like Christ. Henry Knight writes, "Wesley corrected the pervasive notion that Christian salvation is solely about our postmortem destiny, insisting instead it is about receiving a new life in the present, one that lasts through all eternity."[32] The idea of bringing heaven to Earth was not foreign to Wesley, and he believed it will happen as Christians become more like Christ.

WILLIAM CAREY

The Great Awakening produced one of the greatest missional movements of God in all of church history: the Protestant Missionary Movement. William Carey, a confident man known as the father of the modern missionary, believed the gospel was to be taken throughout the earth. In the course of his life, William Carey set a pattern and a standard for missionary work that, in the years since his death, many have copied, but few have matched.[33] His bold belief was the Great Commission was still relevant in his time, a contention that received a less-than-enthusiastic response from a world that largely insisted the Great Commission had been given for the first century only.[34]

His theology was similarly (and often singularly) motivated by grace for all through faith, as evidenced by his favorite Scripture passage, Romans 10:11–13, which says, "'Anyone who believes in him will never be put to

---

30. Wesley, "General Spread of the Gospel," 7.
31. Wesley, "Signs of the Times," 5.
32. Knight, *John Wesley*, 141.
33. Benge and Benge, *William Carey*, loc. 2497 of 2669.
34. Stanley, "Winning the World," para. 5.

shame." For there is no difference between Jew and Gentile—the same Lord is Lord of all and richly blesses all who call on him." Carey's hospitable and optimistic philosophy can be summed up in a quote from a sermon he preached called "Deathless": "Expect great things from God and attempt great things for God."[35]

CHARLES FINNEY

During the Second Great Awakening, Charles Finney, who lived from 1792 to 1875 and possessed similar eschatological beliefs to those of Jonathan Edwards, "preached that if Christians would make themselves useful to the highest degree, revivals and reforms would bring in the millennium."[36] Having concluded Christ would return after the millennium, Christians of the nineteenth century believed they could speed the return of Christ by leading the world to Christ. Because slavery was seen as sinful, this post-millennial belief led a movement of Christians who fought for the abolition of that sinful practice.

The incredible growth of "voluntary societies" can be traced to the eschatology of the leaders of the Second Great Awakening.[37] "Although it may seem far-fetched today, in the first half of the nineteenth century, this grand optimism inspired the Christians to combine evangelism and social reform."[38] In addition to organizing voluntary societies and distributing literature, they built churches, schools, and hospitals.[39] Their commitment to social reform, generated by optimism that the world would be in existence to enjoy such reforms, would spark the founding of many charitable organization and social justice movements.[40] The "benevolent empire" created by the Second Great Awakening was the most robust effort to meet the social challenges of the nineteenth century.[41]

---

35. Graves, "William Carey Preached Deathless Sermon," para. 1.

36. Koester, *Introduction to the History of Christianity*, 72.

37. Noll, *History of Christianity*, 169.

38. Koester, *Introduction to the History of Christianity*, 72.

39. Koester, *Introduction to the History of Christianity*, 65.

40. Noll, *History of Christianity*, 169.

41. Gaustad and Schmidt, *Religious History of America*, 140.

WILLIAM SEYMOUR

The Azusa Street Revival, led by William Seymour, brought together blacks, whites, Hispanics, and Asians to worship with levels of excitement the church in America had never seen.[42] This was frowned upon in the "Jim Crow" era, but the revival broke through that noise. The Pentecostal formula of worship that has become so connected to the Azusa Street Revival included African American heritage, holiness (Methodism) theology, and speaking in tongues. These were the memorable signs of this exuberant, round-the-clock revival. There were some who found the "holy ghost bedlam" and mixing of races offensive, but they were quickly snubbed by the excitement produced by the revival.[43]

After the death of Seymour, the movement began to divide, as Pentecostalism became "fraught with internal tension."[44] However, this division did not stop the growth of Pentecostalism. In fact, their spreading caused it to grow more. The primary appeal of Pentecostalism was not about a specific issue or belief. Instead, it focused on a special quality of experience and an encounter with God. It brought joy and hope to people who struggled to find those feelings elsewhere.

DWIGHT L. MOODY

In the late 1800s, a revivalist with a common touch named Dwight L. Moody innovated evangelism in the Christian church. "With his boundless physical energy, natural shrewdness, self-confidence, and eternal optimism, Dwight Lyman Moody could have become a Gilded Age industrial giant like John D. Rockefeller or Jay Gould. Instead, he became one of the great evangelists of the nineteenth century."[45] He attracted children to his ministry with candy and pony rides, and he drew in adults with music and English classes. He once said, "If you can really make a man believe you love him, you have won him."[46]

---

42. Koester, *Introduction to the History of Christianity*, 196.

43. Koester, *Introduction to the History of Christianity*, 197.

44. Koester, *Introduction to the History of Christianity*, 197.

45. Galli and Olsen, *131 Christians Everyone Should Know*, 70.

46. Galli and Olsen, *131 Christians Everyone Should Know*, 71.

E. STANLEY JONES

In 1954, a revolutionary missionary named E. Stanley Jones preached a sermon titled "How are We to Be Changed?" In that sermon, he told a story about a preacher who preached for 10 weeks about how to avoid nervous breakdowns. Soon after that series of sermons, that pastor had a nervous breakdown. About that, Jones said,

> Whatever gets your attention gets you, and you become like that at which you habitually gaze. So getting your eyes on the right place is everything . . . If you concentrate for 10 weeks on how to avoid a nervous breakdown, you'll probably end in having one . . . He should have turned to the positive side and talked about how to live victoriously. Then the victory side of things would have gotten him.[47]

It was this focus on "the positive side" that drew Jones's followers to Jesus as the divine "yes" rather than a "no."[48] Jones pointed out "the mood of the present day is cynicism. Many people are soured by life . . . And it is turning out badly and sadly, for you can't live by a No. You have to live by a Yes."[49]

BILLY GRAHAM

In the 1950s, more than 214 million people heard the gospel message from Billy Graham, one of most influential individuals in Christian history.[50] This confident and optimistic leader relied on the simple and consistent message of repentance and salvation. His "positive thinking fit well into the 1950s—the Depression was over, the war had been won, and people longed to pursue their own dreams."[51] Under the preaching of Billy Graham, it was excitement for God's grace that drove almost 3 million people to respond to the invitation to repent and be saved.[52] Graham's straightforward message of a loving heavenly Father who would forgive people who had committed great atrocities led a generation of people who had readopted the

47. Jones, "How are We to Be Changed?," 4:10—5:40.

48. Jones, *Divine Yes.*

49. Jones, *Divine Yes*, 14.

50. Grossman, "Billy Graham Reached Millions," para. 16.

51. Koester, *Introduction to the History of Christianity*, 245.

52. Gilbreath and Harrell, "Billy Graham," para. 2.

consumption of alcohol after prohibition to repent of their sins. Some may argue the thesis of this book is overstated, that what the church really needs is a more accurate and thorough presentation of the gospel, but it is difficult to argue that a person could give a more accurate and thorough presentation of the gospel than that which was given by Billy Graham.

OTHER OPTIMISTIC REVIVALISTS

Not every Christian who played a key role in sparking revival can easily be described as an optimist, but most of them can. There have been Christian leaders who have drawn people to God by pointing to his wrath because fear sells, but most church growth has been sparked by optimistic leaders. The most notable character trait of Karl Barth was his courage, but he was also known for the theological virtue of "optimistic and confident liberalism."[53] William Wilberforce was so optimistic he was even initially considered naïve. "He expressed 'no doubt' about his chances of quick success."[54] Walter Rauschenbusch, the man who popularized the social gospel, "was an optimist. He never believed society could become perfect, but he saw humankind as progressing swiftly toward the kingdom."[55]

CAUSATION OF REVIVAL

What will the next great revival of the Christian church look like? A thorough study of the great revivals of the past reveals there are only a few commonalities among all of them, and a few more commonalities among most of them. "There are certain elements of permanency which have been characteristic of all true revivals from Pentecost down to the present time. An analysis of the great revivals of history shows these elements to be prayer, the outpouring of the Holy Spirit, and the presentation of the gospel."[56]

53. "Karl Barth," para. 32.
54. Galli and Olsen, *131 Christians Everyone Should Know*, 284.
55. Galli and Olsen, *131 Christians Everyone Should Know*, 304.
56. Beardsley, *History of American Revivals*, loc. 3105 of 3153.

The Holy Spirit

Although we are called to preach the gospel, it is the Lord who draws people to himself and grows their faith to maturity. Leonard Sweet points out that, "[a]s in Jesus' parable of the seeds, planting frees us to be extravagant in love, yet leaves the results for God to germinate and grow."[57] This implies it is our responsibility to prayerfully respond to the promptings of the Holy Spirit that lead us to evangelize in the right time to the right people. Those promptings are a direct result of the power received from the Holy Spirit. Acts 1:8 shows Christians are on a mission to be God's witnesses. Paul encourages the Galatians to "keep in step with the Spirit" (Gal 5:25). Christians should participate with the Holy Spirit who is within them, but cynicism poses a threat to our recognition of the promptings of the Spirit.

Communication and Technology

The addition of communication technologies on a scale the world has never seen should be a source of great optimism for revival. One contributing factor to most of history's great revivals was communication and technology advancements that led to an increased ability to communicate the gospel message. The ability to speak many languages empowered the church of Acts to make disciples of all nations soon after they were called to do so (Matt 28:16–20). "As the Roman Empire played a major part in preparing the world for the arrival of Jesus Christ, in a similar way, major advancements in technology and new discoveries in science and industry helped to prepare the stage for the dawning of the Reformation."[58] The printing press played a key role in sparking and spreading both the Reformation and the Great Awakening.[59] The Bible was the first book printed with Gutenberg's world-changing, movable-type printing press. This led to the affordable availability of the Bible for the masses.[60] Print media has continued to play a key role in almost every revival in history.

The World War Two Revival (1935–1950), largely led by leaders such as Billy Graham, J. Edwin Orr, Stuart Hamblin, and Jim Vaus, would not

---

57. Sweet, *Nudge*, 23.

58. Moore, *Revival*, 213.

59. McAuley, *Print Technology in Scotland and America*, 95.

60. Sweet, *Viral*, 5.

have been as widespread without radio evangelism.[61] Television has yet to play a major role in a great revival; neither has the internet since it changed our world by moving "from just information (1.0) to interaction and connectivity (2.0) and became a dialogue, not a monologue."[62] Leonard Sweet argues social media is "poised to ignite revival" because of its ability to use words not for the sake of the words themselves but for expressing ideas, sharing news, telling stories, and developing relationships.[63] Avid users of social media use it to find and maintain connection with each other, and this connection has the potential to lead to open dialogue about important topics. Sweet believes it is more natural to incarnate the gospel in TGIF (Twitter, Google, Instagram, Facebook) Culture than in the world of the Gutenbergers (those who are focused on words).[64]

OPTIMISM FOR AMERICAN REVIVAL

Most Christians in the West struggle to find confidence in the viability of Christian revival. "To most, revival is no more than a dream," but that must change because anticipation of revival is an important step in beginning the process of preparing and praying for it.[65] The excitement of kingdom growth drives dedicated disciples of Christ to pursue evangelism on a grand scale. The methods used to fan the flames of revival and awaken souls to their need of revival will change, but the Christian unity and healing that results will be consistent. A common thread of optimistic expectation of revival is found throughout history in the people God used to most effectively spread his gospel.

DISCUSSION QUESTIONS:

a. Take some time to talk about what it would have been like to have experienced the events of Pentecost in Acts 2.

b. As love becomes mature, it becomes sacrificial. Give a description of sacrificial love.

61. "S. Parkes Cadman Dies in Coma at 71."
62. Schultz, *Why Nobody Wants*, loc. 1974 of 4116.
63. Sweet, *Viral*, 13.
64. Sweet, *Viral*, 18.
65. Hulse, *Let's Pray for Global Revival*, 22.

c. When Jesus told his disciples to pray "Thy kingdom come," what did he mean by that phrase? What does it mean for the kingdom of God to "come?"

d. What is the most effective way Christians can sacrificially bring people to Christ?

Conclusion

Hope for the Future Leads to a Hopeful Future

POSITIVITY PRODUCES PASSION FOR progress. Negativity produces fear and disconnection. So far, the desire for Christians to be known more for what we are for rather than for what we are against has not pierced the selfish, human desire to make everyone else in the world look and act like we do. We can't underestimate how much that has damaged our reputation. We aren't seen as the hospitable and graceful people you would assume Jesus' followers would be. We can say we want to be known for what we are for, but we should then follow it up by saying what exactly it is we will stop being against. We have to be for more than just filling seats, building big buildings, and impressing peers. Our passion for the gospel should be obvious. Our excitement about the life-giving power of a relationship with God should be irresistible. Our grateful joy for the lives we get to live should make pre-Christians desire to follow the one who taught us how to truly live and become who God created us to be.

In the same way Nehemiah told the tired temple builders to allow the joy of the Lord to be their strength, the church should spur Christians on with the confidence that comes from knowing God will be victorious. My brother, Billy Wilson, told me "the greatest attribute of a good leader could be resilience." He reminded me of an experience in which we heard Bill Self, the great coach of the Kansas Jayhawks, respond to a question right after he fell short of making it to the Final Four in 2007. The interviewer asked if it was hard to gear up for another run after such a disappointment. Self replied, "If you're a true competitor, you don't have a choice." The next year, Bill Self took the Kansas Jayhawks back to the Final Four, but this time he didn't have to respond to questions about failure because the Kansas Jayhawks won it all. Optimism produces perseverance.

Who are the "true competitors" in God's kingdom? They are the eternal optimists among us. They are the pastors who partner with pastors from other denominations to tell a community Jesus loves them. They are the saints, like my friend Joy, who play on the worship team because they know it reaches young people even though they don't really like the style of music. They are prayer warriors, like my friend Richard, who demonstrate the Christian mission is worth sacrificing for. They are the lay evangelists, like my friend Lyle, who see every pre-Christian as a future child of God, even if they don't know it yet. They are the Sunday school teachers, like my friend June, who write letters with their students to people in prison, encouraging them with messages of God's unconditional love. They are the church board members, like my friend Jim, who push us to believe we can reach more young people with the gospel. God is the prototypical optimist, and look at his track record. Christians, follow his lead.

Time and time again, the church gets distracted by the pharisaical desire to make everyone in the world conform to our standards before they even believe in him who we claim made those standards, and many of those standards are conjured with little biblical support. In fear of swinging the pendulum too far away from living moral lives, we cling to our rules like the Pharisees, forcing healthy living on a world of people who would be drawn to the guidance of Scripture if they first surrendered to its Author. We must not see ourselves as the morality police but as the proclaimers of good news—the best news. If we are driven by our disdain for the behavior of those we hope to reach, the credibility of our "come as you are" messaging will be lost. It will drive people away, and it will fulfill our prophecy of the demise of the church.

If, however, we cast a vision of hope and peace, we will catch the attention of the world, because that is what they desire most. If we can show the world Jesus makes our lives better, and he makes us better at life, we can appeal to their desire for advancement and growth. A positive church is an irresistible church.

ASSURED LONGEVITY

If negativity caused the church to abandon optimistic theologies, can positivity open our minds to the possibility that optimistic theologies are at least an option for consideration? The optimistic church of the future will take a cue from Jonathan Edwards who had a spirit of excitement for the future of the church rather than anger at and seclusion from pre-Christians. It will graciously reach out to millennials and Generation Z with hospitable language they can understand while being less distracted by arguments about secondary theologies and political concerns, and it will allow optimism itself to open its eyes to the full range of future evangelistic possibilities.

After he created the world, God stepped back and called it good, as if to say, "now watch it work." He rested and allowed its beauty to sustain and to amaze, but he did not then leave it alone. The Creator is absolutely involved with the evolution of his creation, and his plan will come to pass. Nothing will hinder its fulfillment. Isaiah 46:9–10 says,

> Remember the former things, those of long ago; I am God, and there is no other; I am God, and there is none like me. I make known the end from the beginning, from ancient times, what is still to come. I say: My purpose will stand, and I will do all that I please.

A positive, optimistic message can and will aid in the reversal of the struggles of the American Christian church that is built on the solid foundations of Jesus Christ, who assured its longevity. Jesus says, "the gates of Hades will not overcome it" (Matt 16:18). Christian theologians who deny the hopeful message of Scripture are leading their Christian followers to unnecessary failure because their belief in inevitable failure has decreased their chances of success.

The numerical slowdown of the church in America should not be seen as a predictor of the future, prophesied by either Old Testament or New Testament prophets. There is plenty of reason to believe the Christian church in the United States will see a revival, even soon, and that optimism itself could actually be part of the solution the church is looking for. When the church became militant toward and angry at the world, it caused the world to see the church in a very different way than it saw Jesus. The good news is the youngest generations are ready to hear Jesus' message of hope and grace, and the hope that is caused by knowing there is reason to be optimistic about the future will actually develop positivity that will help the church achieve the goal of the Great Commission.

WHERE WE GO FROM HERE

I have now told two stories about Life.Church (previously LifeChurch.tv). If you'll allow me, I'd like to tell a third. In the year 2000, when the elders of MetroChurch in Edmond, Oklahoma made the kingdom-minded decision to become part of the Life.Church congregation, the pastor of Life. Church, Craig Groeschel, made the optimistic decision to try something he had never seen succeed: he launched a second campus. That brave decision has not only played a huge role in making Life.Church one of the largest churches in the world, it also changed the way many churches think about reaching new people. At the time of the expansion, Groeschel said, "The church needs to adapt, to provide people with options of times, locations and worship options."[1] Groeschel later said, "There's an epidemic of negativity around the world . . . I'm not optimistic based on what I feel. I'm optimistic based on what God says."[2] He recently preached a teaching series called "Stay Positive." The description of that series includes the following: "Cynicism and negativity may be the easy choice, but they're not the best choice. If you seek what's good, you'll see what's good. Let's embrace the way we're created to think and stay positive."[3]

Optimism can open avenues for future church growth by producing confidence, as it does in the best entrepreneurs. When Paul made the unpopular decision to extend the Christian invitation to the gentiles, he expanded the reach of Christianity (Acts 9:15). When the printing press was used to make the Bible more readily available, the world became more aware of the Christian message.[4] The church grew when Whitefield and Wesley broke with the norm by investing in field preaching.[5] When optimistic Christians do what is out of the ordinary because they believe it can produce growth of the body of Christ, they participate in the advancement of the Great Commission.

The Christian who risks his or her reputation to try something unpopular to produce the next great Christian revival will not be a pessimist. The congregation that discovers how to reach Generation Z with the gospel message on a large scale will not be pastored by a person who is

---

1. Ross, "MetroChurch Members," 24.

2. Kumar, "Pastor Craig Groeschel Shares 8 Biblical Reasons," para. 7.

3. Life.Church, "Stay Positive," para. 1.

4. Kennedy, "What Impact?," para. 5.

5. Singleton, "At the Roots of Methodism," para. 11.

overwhelmed by cynicism. The next Martin Luther will see potential when others fear change. The next Jonathan Edwards will believe the Great Commission is achievable, and the next Billy Graham will believe Jesus' promise that nothing can overcome his church (Matt 16:18).

Appendix A

Pastor Survey Results

Answer Choices	Responses (Percent- age)	Responses (Count)
Hostility toward Christianity in the world is increasing.	81.36%	48
Sinfulness is the world is increasing.	69.49%	41
Violence in the world is increasing.	62.71%	37
Hostility toward Christianity will continue to increase until Jesus returns.	69.49%	41
Sinfulness will continue to increase until Jesus returns.	64.41%	38
Violence will continue to increase until Jesus returns.	54.24%	32
Hostility toward Christianity in the world is decreasing.	8.47%	5
Sinfulness in the world is decreasing.	3.39%	2
Violence in the world is decreasing.	11.86%	7
Hostility toward Christianity will continue to decrease until Jesus returns.	1.69%	1
Sinfulness will continue to decrease until Jesus returns.	1.69%	1
Violence will continue to decrease until Jesus returns.	3.39%	2
Total Respondents: 59		

Appendix B
Eschatology Theories

Eschatology Theories

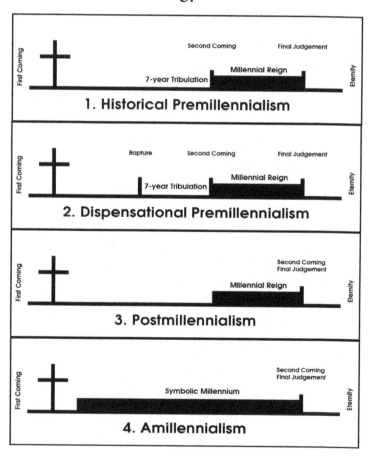

1. Historical Premillennialism

2. Dispensational Premillennialism

3. Postmillennialism

4. Amillennialism

Bibliography

Achor, Shawn. *Before Happiness: The 5 Hidden Keys to Achieving Success, Spreading Happiness, and Sustaining Positive Change*. New York: Random House, 2013.

———. *The Happiness Advantage: The Seven Principles that Fuel Success and Performance at Work*. New York: Virgin, 2011.

Ahola, Kirsi, et al. "Work-Related Exhaustion and Temomere Length: A Population-Based Study." *PLOS ONE* 7.7 (2012) 1–7. https://doi.org/10.1371/journal.pone.0040186.

Alcorn, Randy. "C.S. Lewis on Heaven and the New Earth: God." *Desiring God*, September 28, 2013. https://www.desiringgod.org/messages/c-s-lewis-on-heaven-and-the-new-earth-god-s-eternal-remedy-to-the-problem-of-evil-and-suffering.

Allen, Bob. "Millennials Losing Their Religion." *Baptist News Global*, June 25, 2012. http://www.abpnews.com/culture/social-issues/item/7555-millennials-losing-their-religion.html.

Altrogge, Stephen, "What is This World Coming to? Exactly What Jesus Said it Would." https://www.biblestudytools.com/blogs/stephen-altrogge/what-is-this-world-coming-to-exactly-what-jesus-said-it-would-come-to.html.

American Psychiatric Association. "Americans Say They are More Anxious than a Year Ago; Baby Boomers Report Greatest Increase in Anxiety." May 7, 2018. https://www.psychiatry.org/newsroom/news-releases/americans-say-they-are-more-anxious-than-a-year-ago-baby-boomers-report-greatest-increase-in-anxiety.

Aoun, Joseph E. "Innovation Imperative: Enhancing the Talent Pipeline." *News@ Northeastern*. April 30, 2014. https://president.northeastern.edu/2014/04/30/inno%C2%ADva%C2%ADtion-imper%C2%ADa%C2%ADtive-enhancing-the-talent-pipeline/.

Apple. "iPhone to Support Third-Party Web 2.0 Applications." June 11, 2007. https://www.apple.com/newsroom/2007/06/11iPhone-to-Support-Third-Party-Web-2-0-Applications/.

Avolio, Bruce J., et al. "Leadership: Current Theories, Research, and Future Directions." *Annual Review of Psychology* 60.1 (2009) 421–49.

Axton, Paul. "Escaping an Evil Christianity: Must Theological Education Go Underground?" *Forging Ploughshares*, June 30, 2018. https://forgingploughshares.org/2018/06/30/escaping-an-evil-christianity-must-theological-education-go-underground/.

———. "Homeless Christianity: The Church Militant or Triumphant? Part II." *Forging Ploughshares*, August 16, 2018. https://forgingploughshares.org/2018/08/16/homeless-christianity-the-church-militant-or-triumphant-part-ii/.

Ayoud, Justin L. "Harold Camping Oct. 21 Rapture: Westboro Baptist Church to Protest 6B Funerals." *The Christian Post*, October 21, 2011. https://www.christianpost.com/news/harold-camping-oct-21-rapture-westboro-baptist-church-to-protest-6b-funerals-59009/.

Aziz, John, "Less Racism and Sexism Means More Economic Growth." *The Week*, December 16, 2013. https://theweek.com/articles/454335/less-racism-sexism-means-more-economic-growth.

Banks, David. "Image of Grace: Seeing and Sharing the Gospel through Imagery." DMin diss., Portland Seminary, 2012. http://digitalcommons.georgefox.edu/dmin/31.

Barna, George. "Christianity Has a Strong Positive Image Despite Fewer Active Participants." *Barna Group*, February 5, 1996. http://www.barna.org/cgi-bin/PagePressRelease.asp?PressReleaseID=34.

The Barna Group. "Americans are Exploring New Ways of Experiencing God." June 8, 2009. https://www.barna.com/research/americans-are-exploring-new-ways-of-experiencing-god/.

———. "What People Experience in Churches." January 9, 2012. http://www.barna.org/congregations-articles/556-what-people-experience-in-churches.html.

Barrick, Audrey. "Poll: What Evangelical Leaders Believe about the End Times." *The Christian Post*, March 9, 2011. https://www.christianpost.com/news/poll-what-evangelical-leaders-believe-about-the-end-times-49340/.

Beardsley, Frank G. *A History of American Revivals*. Kansas City, KS: American Tract Society, 2012. Kindle.

Ben-Shahar, Tal, and Angus Ridgway. *The Joy of Leadership: How Positive Psychology Can Maximize Your Impact (and Make You Happier) in a Challenging World*. Hoboken, NJ: Wiley & Sons, 2017.

Benge, Janet, and Geoff Benge. *William Carey: Obliged to Go, Christian Heroes: Then and Now*. Seattle: YWAM, 2011. Kindle.

Bershidsky, Leonid. "Here Comes Generation Z." *Bloomberg*, June 18, 2014. https://www.bloomberg.com/view/articles/2014-06-18/nailing-generation-z.

Bertholet, Rodney F. "These Dead Bones Can Rise Again: Preventing Church Closures in North America." DMin diss., Portland Seminary, 2013. http://digitalcommons.georgefox.edu/dmin/41.

Binker, Mark. "Newspaper Confirms Obama Not the AntiChrist." *WRAL*, July 13, 2015. https://www.wral.com/newspaper-confirms-obama-not-the-antichrist/14450321/.

Boda, Mark J., and J. Gordon McConville, eds. *Dictionary of the Old Testament: Prophets*. Downers Grove, IL: InterVarsity, 2012.

Boettner, Loraine. *Postmillennialism*. Self-published, Amazon Digital Services, 2011. Kindle.

Branstetter, C. J. *Purity, Power, and Pentecostal Light: The Revivalist Doctrine and Means of Aaron Merritt Hills*. Eugene, OR: Pickwick, 2012.

Bromwich, Jonah Engel, "Generation X More Addicted to Social Media than Millennials, Report Finds." *New York Times*, January 27, 2017. https://www.nytimes.com/2017/01/27/technology/millennial-social-media-usage.html.

Brown, Charis Hillman. "Why Christianity Has an Image Problem." 7 Cultural Mountains, http://www.7culturalmountains.org/Blog/Theology-of-the-7-Mountains/Theology-of-the-7-Mountains/Christianity-Has-An-Image-Problem&fldKeywords=&fldAuthor=&fldTopic=0.

Bruner, Frederick Dale. *A Theology of the Holy Spirit: The Pentecostal Experience and the New Testament Witness*. Unicoi, TN: Trinity Foundation, 2001.

Bryant, M. Darrol, and Donald W. Dayton. *The Coming Kingdom: Essays in American Millennialism & Eschatology*. Barrytown, NY: International Religious Foundation, 1983.

Burke, John. *No Perfect People Allowed: Creating a Come as You are Culture in the Church*. Grand Rapids: Zondervan, 2006.

Buser, Sam, et al. "Depression & PTSD Shown to Be Strongest Predictors of Firefighter Suicide." *Firehouse.com*, November 25, 2016. http://www.firehouse.com/article/12280354/depression-ptsd-shown-to-be-strongest-predictors-of-firefighter-suicide.

Buttrick, George Arthur, ed. *The Interpreter's Dictionary of the Bible Volume 3 K-Q: An Illustrated Encyclopedia Identifying and Explaining All Proper Names and Significant Terms and Subjects in the Holy Scriptures, including the Apocrypha*. New York: Abingdon, 1962.

Carey, Brycchan. "Slavery Timeline 1501–1600. A Chronology of Slavery, Abolition, and Emancipation." http://www.brycchancarey.com/slavery/chrono3.htm.

Cathail, Maidhc O. "The Scofield Bible—The Book that Made Zionists of America's Evangelical Christians." *Washington Report on Middle East Affairs*, September 24, 2015. https://www.wrmea.org/2015-october/the-scofield-bible-the-book-that-made-zionists-of-americas-evangelical-christians.html.

CBS News. "Starbucks CEO Howard Schultz is All Abuzz." June 5, 2012. http://www.cbsnews.com/news/starbucks-ceo-howard-schultz-is-all-abuzz/.

Chabris, Christopher F., and Daniel J. Simons. *The Invisible Gorilla: And Other Ways Our Intuitions Deceive Us*. New York: MJF, 2012.

Chaves, Mark, et al. "The National Congregations Study: Background, Methods, and Selected Results." *Journal for the Scientific Study of Religion* 38.4 (December 1999) 458–76.

Chesterton, G. K. *Orthodoxy*. Garden City, NY: Image, 1959.

Cliff, Gareth. "This is the Best Time to Be Alive." Lecture filmed August 1, 2015, at University of Free State. TEDx video. 19:19. https://youtu.be/W-I3w7U8H8s.

Collins, Jim. *Good to Great: Why Some Companies Make the Leap . . . and Others Don't*. London: Random House, 2001.

Craig, William Lane, "#439 Christian Pessimism?" *Reasonable Faith*, September 13, 2015. https://www.reasonablefaith.org/question-answer/P100/christian-pessimism.

Curran, Thomas, and Andrew P. Hill. "Perfectionism is Increasing Over Time: A Meta-Analysis of Birth Cohort Differences From 1989 to 2016." *Psychological Bulletin*, December 28, 2017. https://www.apa.org/pubs/journals/releases/bul-bul0000138.pdf.

Darabont, Frank, dir. *The Shawshank Redemption*. 1994; Culver City, CA: Columbia Pictures, 1994. DVD.

Darby, J. N. "On the Formation of Churches, Further Developments." *The Collected Writings of J. N. Darby*, Eccl. 1, Vol. 1, edited by William Kelly, 1:138–55. 47 vols. Kingston-on-Thames, UK: Stow Hill Bible and Trust Depot, 1962.

———. "What is the Unity of the Church?" *The Collected Writings of J. N. Darby*, Eccl. 4, Vol. 20, edited by William Kelly, 296–305. 29 vols. Kingston-on-Thames: Stow Hill Bible and Trust Depot, 1962.

Dawson, Christopher. "The Six Ages of the Church." In *Christianity and European Culture*, edited by Gerald J. Russello, 34–45. Washington, DC: Catholic University of America Press, 1998.

Daykin, Jerry. "Five Things Great Brands Will Do Differently on Social Media in 2015." *The Guardian*, December 22, 2014. https://www.theguardian.com/media-network/2014/dec/22/brands-social-media-marketing-2015.

Dayton, Donald W. *Methodism & the Fragmentation of American Protestantism, 1865–1920*. Wilmore, KY: Asbury Theological Seminary Press, 1995.

DeMar, Gary. "Why Bother if the End is Near?" *American Vision*, January 8, 2016. https://americanvision.org/3514/why-bother-if-the-end-is-near/#identifier_6_3514.

DeSilva, David Arthur. *An Introduction to the New Testament: Contexts, Methods & Ministry Formation*. Downers Grove, IL: InterVarsity, 2004.

Domonoske, Camila, "Tim LaHaye, Evangelical Legend Behind 'Left Behind' Series, Dies at 90." *NPR*, July 25, 2016. https://www.npr.org/sections/thetwo-way/2016/07/25/487382209/tim-lahaye-evangelical-legend-behind-left-behind-series-dies-at-90.

Drury, John. "Lecture 8.1, Intro to Christian Theology THEO-500." Wesley Seminary at Indiana Wesleyan University. Marion, Indiana, December 10, 2018.

Eberle, Harold R., and Martin Trench. *Victorious Eschatology: A Partial Preterist View*. Yakima, WA: Worldcast, 2009.

Edwards, Jonathan. "A Faithful Narrative of the Surprising Work of God." http://www.jonathan-edwards.org/Narrative.html.

———. *A Humble Attempt to Promote Explicit Agreement and Visible Union of God's People, in Extraordinary Prayer, for the Revival of Religion and the Advancement*. Edited by Henry Rogers and Edward Hickman. Self-published, Amazon Digital Servics, 2011. Kindle.

———. *Jonathan Edwards: Writings from the Great Awakening*. Edited Philip F. Gura. New York: Library of America, 2013. Kindle.

Edwards, Jonathan. *The Works of Jonathan Edwards, A.M. Edited by* Edward Hickman. London: Henry G. Bohn, 1865.

Elliot, Andrew J., and Todd M. Thrash. "Approach-avoidance Motivation in Personality: Approach and Avoidance Temperaments and Goals." *Journals of Personality and Social Psychology* 82 (2002) 804–18.

Emmons, Robert A. *Thanks!: How the New Science of Gratitude Can Make You Happier*. Boston: Houghton Mifflin, 2007.

Encyclopædia Britannica. "William Miller." https://www.britannica.com/biography/William-Miller.

Erickson, Erick. "I Increasingly Find Conflict between My Faith and Some Conservative Discourse." *The Resurgent*, August 21, 2014. https://theresurgent.com/2014/08/21/i-increasingly-find-conflict-between-my-faith-and-some-conservative-discourse/.

Erickson, Millard J. *A Basic Guide to Eschatology: Making Sense of the Millennium*. Grand Rapids: Baker Academic, 1998.

Escobedo-Frank, Dottie. "The Church Revolution from the Edge." DMin diss., Portland Seminary, 2012. https://digitalcommons.georgefox.edu/dmin/34.

EyeWitness to History. "Nero Persecutes the Christians, 64 A.D." 2000. http://www.eyewitnesstohistory.com/christians.htm.

Fea, John. "Is Robert Jeffress Really a Bigot?" *The Way of Improvement Leads Home*, May 17, 2018. https://thewayofimprovement.com/2018/05/17/is-robert-jeffress-really-a-bigot/.

———. "The Strategic Implications of American Millennialism." *The Way of Improvement Leads Home*, May 24, 2018. https://thewayofimprovement.com/2018/05/24/the-strategic-implications-of-american-millennialism/.

Fredrickson, Barbara L. "The Broaden-and-Build Theory of Positive Emotions." *Philosophical Transactions of the Royal Society B: Biological Sciences* 359 (2004) 1366–77.

———. *Positivity: Groundbreaking Research Reveals How to Embrace the Hidden Strength of Positive Emotions, Overcome Negativity, and Thrive.* New York: Crown, 2009.

———. "The Role of Positive Emotions in Positive Psychology: The Broaden-and-build Theory of Positive Emotions." *American Psychologist* 56 (2001) 218–26.

Galli, Mark, and Ted Olsen. *131 Christians Everyone Should Know.* Nashville: Holman Reference, 2000.

Gallo, Carmine. "5 Reasons Why Optimists Make Better Leaders." *Forbes*, August 8, 2012. https://www.forbes.com/sites/carminegallo/2012/08/08/5-reasons-why-optimists-make-better-leaders/.

Garner, Duane. *Why the End is Not Near (Answers in an Hour).* Monroe, LA: Athanasius, 2008. Kindle.

Gaustad, Edwin S., and Leigh Eric Schmidt. *The Religious History of America.* San Francisco: HarperOne, 2009.

Gentry, Kenneth L., Jr. "2 Tim 3 (# 8) Despair or Hope?" *Postmillennial Worldview.* January 28, 2015. https://postmillennialworldview.com/2015/01/28/2-tim-3-or-the-postmillennial-hope-8/#more-5857.

Geraghty, Jim, "There are a Lot of Reasons to Feel Optimistic about America's Future." *National Review*, August 3, 2018. https://www.nationalreview.com/the-morning-jolt/america-future-optimism-warranted/.

Gibson, Scott M., and A. J. Gordon. *American Premillennialist.* Lanham, MD: University Press of America, 2001.

Gilbreath, Edward, and David Harrell. "Billy Graham." http://www.christianitytoday.com/history/people/evangelistsandapologists/billy-graham.html.

Gill, Anthony. "Religious Liberty and Economic Prosperity: Four Lessons from the Past." *Cato Journal* 37 (Winter 2017) 115–34. https://object.cato.org/sites/cato.org/files/serials/files/cato-journal/2017/2/cj-v37n1-9.pdf.

Gledhill, Ruth. "Exclusive: New Figures Reveal Massive Decline in Religious Affiliation." *Christian Today*, October 17, 2014. http://www.christiantoday.com/article/exclusive.new.figures.reveal.massive.decline.in.religious.affiliation/41799.htm.

Goldfarb, Lyn, and Margaret Koval. "Roman Empire in the First Century, The 4x55." http://pbsinternational.org/programs/roman-empire-in-the-first-century-the/.

Gordon, A. J. *The Holy Spirit in Missions.* New York: Revell, 1893.

Graves, Dan. "William Carey Preached Deathless Sermon." *Christianity.com*, July 2007. http://www.christianity.com/church/church-history/timeline/1701-1800/william-carey-preached-deathless-sermon-11630317.html.

Grossman, Cathy Lynn. "Billy Graham Reached Millions through His Crusades. Here's How He Did it." *USA Today*, February 21, 2018. https://www.usatoday.com/story/news/nation/2018/02/21/billy-graham-crusades-how-evangelists-reached-millions/858165001/.

———. "Most Religious Groups in USA Have Lost Ground, Survey Finds." *USA Today*, March 17, 2009. https://usatoday30.usatoday.com/news/religion/2009-03-09-american-religion-ARIS_N.htm.

Guest. "How Digital Technology is Creating a World of Introverts." *Adweek*, July 3, 2013. https://www.adweek.com/digital/how-social-media-is-creating-a-world-of-introverts/.

Guthrie, Donald, et al., eds. *The New Bible Commentary*. Grand Rapids: Eerdmans, 1991.

Hall, Chad. "Leader's Insight: The Disappearing Middle." *CT Pastors*, July 2007. http://www.christianitytoday.com/pastors/2007/july-online-only/cln70716.html.

Hansen, Collin, "We Must Not Play by Majority Rules." *The Gospel Coalition*, March 1, 2016. https://www.thegospelcoalition.org/article/we-must-not-play-by-majority-rules/.

Harrop, Jennie. *The Jesus Quotient: IQ to EQ to AQ*. Eugene, OR: Cascade, 2019.

Hawkins, Greg L., et al. *Reveal*. Barrington, IL: Willow Creek Resources, 2007.

Hawthorne, Gerald F., et al. *Dictionary of Paul and His Letters A Compendium of Contemporary Biblical Scholarship*. Downers Grove, IL: InterVarsity, 2015.

Hewitt, Steve. "Why the Church is Dying in America." *Christian Computing Magazine* (July 1, 2012) 3–5.

Hills, Aaron Merritt. *Fundamental Christian Theology*. Pasadena, CA: C. J. Kinne, 1932.

Hinkle, John Austin, Jr. "A Simple Cup of Coffee: What Starbucks Can Teach the Church about Hospitality in How We Reach Our Neighbors." DMin diss., Portland Seminary, 2015. http://digitalcommons.georgefox.edu/dmin/112.

Hirsch, Alan. "Missional Velocity." Vimeo. April 29, 2010. 47:01. https://vimeo.com/11320693.

Hiscox, Edward T. "Pre-Millennial Theology." *Watchmen* 23 (January 1890) 2.

"History." http://je.yalecollege.yale.edu/about-us/history#sthash.CI9ShfG9.dpuf.

Hulse, Erroll. *Let's Pray for Global Revival*. N.p.: Chapel Library, 2014. Kindle.

Humphrey, Ronald H. *Effective Leadership Theory, Cases, and Applications*. Los Angeles: Sage, 2013.

Ice, Tommy. "A Short History of Dispensationalism." *Worldview Weekend*, November 9, 2015. https://www.worldviewweekend.com/news/article/short-history-dispensationalism.

"Introduction to Dispensationalism." Scofield Biblical Institute. October 25, 2016. http://scofieldinstitute.org/introduction-to-dispensationalism/.

Jackson, Wayne. "When Was the Book of Revelation Written?" *Christian Courier*. https://www.christiancourier.com/articles/1552-when-was-the-book-of-revelation-written.

Jenkins, Philip. *The Next Christendom: The Coming of Global Christianity*. Oxford: Oxford University Press, 2011.

Jenkins, Ryan. "15 Aspects that Highlight How Generation Z is Different from Millennials." http://www.ryan-jenkins.com/2015/06/08/15-aspects-that-highlight-how-generation-z-is-different-from-millennials/.

Jones, E. Stanley. *The Divine Yes*. Nashville: Abingdon, 1975.

———. "How are We to Be Changed?" E. Stanley Jones Foundation, June 1, 2012, M4a audio, 50:06. https://www.estanleyjonesfoundation.com/wp-content/uploads/2012/06/01-How-Are-We-to-be-Changed_-1954.m4a.

Kalish, Emma "Millennials are the Least Wealthy but Most Optimistic Generation." *Urban Institute*, April 2016. https://www.urban.org/sites/default/files/

publication/79881/2000753-Millennials-Are-the-Least-Wealthy-but-Most-Optimistic-Generation.pdf.

"Karl Barth (1886–1968), a detailed Biography." https://www.museeprotestant.org/en/notice/karl-barth-1886-1968-a-detailed-biography/.

Kennedy, Rita. "What Impact Did the Invention of the Printing Press Have on the Spread of Religion?" https://classroom.synonym.com/impact-did-invention-printing-press-spread-religion-6617.html.

Keysers, Christian, et al. "A Touching Sight: SII/PV Activation During the Observation and Experience of Touch." *Neuron* 42.2 (April 22, 2004) 336–46.

Khokunthod, Tiger. "The Problem with Millennials: Entitled, Lazy, Worthless." *The Odyssey Online*, November 28, 2016. https://www.theodysseyonline.com/millennials-are-not-the-problem.

King, Martin Luther, Jr. "Sermon at Temple Israel of Hollywood." http://www.americanrhetoric.com/speeches/mlktempleisraelhollywood.htm.

Kinnaman, David. "Five Trends among the Unchurched." *Barna Group*, October 9, 2014. https://www.barna.com/research/five-trends-among-the-unchurched/.

———. *You Lost Me*: *Why Young Christians are Leaving Church . . . And Rethinking Faith*. Grand Rapids: Baker, 2011. Kindle.

Kinnaman, David, and Gabe Lyons. *Good Faith: Being a Christian When Society Thinks You're Irrelevant and Extreme*. Grand Rapids: Baker, 2016. Kindle.

———. *Unchristian: What a New Generation Really Thinks about Christianity—And Why it Matters*. Grand Rapids: Baker, 2007. Kindle.

Knight, Henry, *John Wesley: Optimist of Grace*. Eugene, OR: Cascade, 2018.

Koester, Nancy. *Introduction to the History of Christianity in the United States*. Minneapolis: Fortress, 2015.

Krupp, Steven, and Paul J. H. Schoemaker. *Winning the Long Game: How Strategic Leaders Shape the Future*. New York: Public Affairs, 2014.

Kuhel, Beth. "Positive People Attract People and Breed Successful Careers." *Personal Branding* (blog), November 10, 2012. http://www.personalbrandingblog.com/positive-people-attract-people-and-breed-successful-careers/.

Kumar, Anugrah. "Pastor Craig Groeschel Shares 8 Biblical Reasons to Be Optimistic." *Christian Post*, September 21, 2015. https://www.christianpost.com/news/lifechurch-tv-pastor-craig-groeschel-shares-8-biblical-reasons-to-be-optimistic.html

Kurschner, Alan. "Randal Rauser Asserts Premillennialism is Pessimistic, Therefore, it is against Social Justice and the Enviroment." *Eschatos Ministries*, January 23, 2013. https://www.alankurschner.com/2013/01/23/randal-rauser-asserts-premillennialism-is-pessimistic-therefore-it-is-against-social-justice-and-the-environment/.

Lane, Robert Edwards. *The Loss of Happiness in Market Democracies*. London: Yale University Press, 2000.

LaPlante, Logan. "Hackschooling Makes Me Happy." Filmed February 12, 2013 at University of Nevada. TEDx video, 11:14. https://www.youtube.com/watch?v=h11u3vtcpaY.

Lapp, Amber, and David Lapp. "A Generation Conflicted about Marriage." https://medium.com/2016-index-of-culture-and-opportunity/a-generation-conflicted-about-marriage-9a5fde4ce096.

Laurie, Greg. "What is the Difference between a Spiritual Awakening and a Revival?" *Crosswalk.com*, July 25, 2018. https://www.crosswalk.com/faith/spiritual-life/what-is-the-difference-between-a-spiritual-awakening-and-a-revival.html.

Leith, John H. *Creeds of the Churches: A Reader in Christian Doctrine From the Bible to Present.* Louisville: Westminster John Knox, 1982.

Lenhart, Amanda, et al. "Teens, Technology and Romantic Relationships." *Pew Research Center,* October 1, 2015. http://www.pewinternet.org/2015/10/01/teens-technology-and-romantic-relationships/.

Lesonsky, Rieva, "The Rise of Gen Z Entrepreneurs." *Bank of America,* June 13, 2019. https://smallbusinessonlinecommunity.bankofamerica.com/community/running-your-business/general-business/blog/2019/06/13/the-rise-of-gen-z-entrepreneurs.

Leviyah, Xenia, et al. "Mood Changes after Brief Exposure to Emotional Information: Positive and Negative Affect Changes in Relation to Visual and Auditory Emotional Information." Poster presented at the Massachusetts Statewide Undergraduate Research Conference, April 28, 2017, Amherst, MA. https://umassbostonbabylab.weebly.com/uploads/6/4/9/3/64936741/umassamherst2017_bethancourt_moodpanas_final.pdf.

Levy, Gabrielle, "Abortion Rates: Where and Why They are Falling," *U.S. News and World Report,* March 21, 2018. https://www.usnews.com/news/data-mine/articles/2018-03-21/abortion-rates-where-and-why-theyre-falling.

Lewis, C. S. *The Last Battle.* London: Collier, 1956.

Lien, Tracey. "Teens Spend an Average of 9 Hours a Day with Media, Survey Finds." *Los Angeles Times,* November 3, 2015. http://www.latimes.com/business/technology/la-fi-tn-teens-television-media-20151103-story.html.

Life.Church. "Stay Positive." https://open.life.church/resources/2126-stay-positive.

Lipman, Victor, "Why a Positive Mindset is a Manager's Indispensable Ally." *Forbes,* October 12, 2017. https://www.forbes.com/sites/victorlipman/2017/10/12/why-a-positive-mindset-is-a-managers-indispensable-ally/#252158d84425.

———. "Why Confidence is Always a Leader's Best Friend." *Forbes,* May 9, 2017. https://www.forbes.com/sites/victorlipman/2017/05/09/why-confidence-is-always-a-leaders-best-friend/#300cc08147be.

Lokkesmoe, Ryan. *Paul and His Team: What the Early Church Can Teach Us about Leadership and Influence.* Chicago: Moody, 2017.

Long, Heather. "56 Percent of Americans Think Their Kids Will Be Worse Off." *CNNMoney,* January 28, 2016. http://money.cnn.com/2016/01/28/news/economy/donald-trump-bernie-sanders-us-economy/index.html.

Love, Ed. "The Coming God: Pursuing a Theology of Hope." DMin diss., Portland Seminary, 2011. http://digitalcommons.georgefox.edu/dmin/5.

Lugo, Luis. "'Nones' on the Rise." *Pew Forum,* October 9, 2012. http://www.pewforum.org/2012/10/09/nones-on-the-rise/.

Lyons, Gabe. "Christianity Has an Image Problem." https://www.preachitteachit.org/articles/detail/christianity-has-an-image-problem/.

Lyubomirsky, Sonja. *The How of Happiness: A Practical Guide to Getting the Life You Want.* London: Piatkus, 2010. Kindle.

Lyubomirsky, Sonja, et al. "The Benefits of Frequent Positive Affect: Does Happiness Lead to Success?" *Psychological Bulletin* 131.6 (2005) 803–55.

MacDonald, Gordon. "Beyond Pessimism or Optimism." *Christianity Today,* January 2009. https://www.christianitytoday.com/pastors/2009/january-online-only/beyondpessimismoptimism.html.

Malamud, Paul, ed. *Human Rights in Brief.* Washington, DC: US Department of State, 2006. https://photos.state.gov/libraries/mongolia/805999/PDFs/Human-Rights-in-Brief.pdf.

Martin, Ralph P., and Peter H. Davids, eds. *Dictionary of the Later New Testament & Its Developments.* Downers Grove, IL: IVP Academic, 1997.

Mataxas, Eric. *Bonhoeffer: Pastor, Martyr, Prophet, Spy.* Nashville: Thomas Nelson, 2011.

Mathew, Shyju, and Tiny Mathew. "Why Does 'Revival,' a Sovereign Act of God, Need an Active Pursuit?" *Revive Nations,* November 10, 2011. https://revivenations.org/blog/2012/11/10/revival-active-pursuit/.

McAuley, Louis Kirk. *Print Technology in Scotland and America: 1740–1800.* Lewisburg, NY: Bucknell University, 2013.

McDurmon, Joel, "An Open Letter to Erick Erickson: Reasons to Dump the Pessimistic Eschatology." *The American Vision,* August, 29, 2014. https://americanvision.org/11275/an-open-letter-to-erick-erickson-time-to-dump-the-pessimistic-eschatology11275/.

McLaren, Brian. *A Generous Orthodoxy: By Celebrating Strengths of Many Traditions in the Church (and Beyond), This Book Will Seek to Communicate a "Generous Orthodoxy."* Grand Rapids: Zondervan, 2004.

McNall, Joshua. *Long Story Short.* Franklin, TN: Seedbed, 2018.

———. "What Seven Thunders Spoke: Why Some Revelations Ought to Go Unpublished." February 8, 2018. https://joshuamcnall.com/2018/02/08/what-seven-thunders-spoke-why-some-revelations-ought-to-go-unpublished/.

"'Millennials on Steroids': Is Your Brand Ready for Generation Z?" *Knowledge@Wharton,* September 28, 2015. http://knowledge.wharton.upenn.edu/article/millennials-on-steroids-is-your-brand-ready-for-generation-z/.

Miller, Stephen M. *The Complete Guide to the Bible.* Phoenix: Barbour, 2007.

Moore, Beth. "Jesus, Come Get Us." Twitter. June 1, 2020, 20:16. https://twitter.com/BethMooreLPM/status/1267641177194614786

Moore, Paul. *Revival—Before and After.* Self-published: Amazon Digital Services, 2015. Kindle.

Mounce, William D. *Pastoral Epistles.* World Biblical Commentary. Nashville: Thomas Nelson, 2000.

Murphy, Matthew L. "Missional Communities: Why They are Failing and How to Help Them Thrive." DMin diss., Portland Seminary, 2017. http://digitalcommons.georgefox.edu/dmin/221.

Murray, Lain. "Jonathan Edwards: The Life, the Man, and the Legacy." *Desiring God,* October 11, 2003. https://www.desiringgod.org/messages/jonathan-edwards-the-life-the-man-and-the-legacy.

Mutch, Christine M. "Sustainable Faith: How the Neuroscience of Emotion Promotes Spiritual Transformation." DMin diss., Portland Seminary, 2014. http://digitalcommons.georgefox.edu/dmin/77.

Myers, Gary D. "Theological Ed. is 'Being Redefined.'" *Baptist Press,* April 20, 2011. http://www.bpnews.net/bpnews.asp?id=35098.

National Archives. "From George Washington to Charles Mynn Thruston, 10 August 1794." *Founders Online,* June 13, 2018. https://founders.archives.gov/documents/Washington/05-16-02-0376.

Neatby, William Blair. *A History of the Plymouth Brethren.* 2nd ed. London: Hodder and Stoughton, 1902.

"The Next Christendom: The Coming of Global Christianity." *Publishers Weekly.* March 1, 2002. https://www.publishersweekly.com/0-19-514616-6.

Noll, Mark A. *A History of Christianity in the United States and Canada.* Grand Rapids: Eerdmans, 2003.

O'Brian, Brandon J. "Christ, Culture, and the Generation Gap." *Christianity Today,* October 23, 2012. https://www.christianitytoday.com/biblestudies/articles/evangelism/generation-gap.html?start=2.

O'Connor, Flannery. "Parker's Back." *Esquire* (April 1, 1965) 76–155.

Ortlund, Dane C. "5 Things Jonathan Edwards Teaches Us about the Christian Life." *Crossway,* August 26, 2014. https://www.crossway.org/articles/5-things-jonathan-edwards-teaches-us-about-the-christian-life/.

Osnos, Evan. "Doomsday Prep for the Super-Rich." *The New Yorker,* August 10, 2017. https://www.newyorker.com/magazine/2017/01/30/doomsday-prep-for-the-super-rich.

Perlstein, Josh. "Engaging Generation Z: Marketing to a New Brand of Consumer." *Adweek,* November 27, 2017. https://www.adweek.com/digital/josh-perlstein-response-media-guest-post-generation-z/.

Pew Research Center. "America's Changing Religious Landscape." May 12, 2015. http://www.pewforum.org/2015/05/12/americas-changing-religious-landscape/.

———. "Jesus Christ's Return to Earth." July 14, 2010. https://www.pewresearch.org/fact-tank/2010/07/14/jesus-christs-return-to-earth/.

———. "Millennials in Adulthood." March 7, 2014. http://www.pewsocialtrends.org/2014/03/07/millennials-in-adulthood/.

———. "Social Media Fact Sheet." January 12, 2017. http://www.pewinternet.org/fact-sheet/social-media/.

Pfeiffer, Charles F., and Everett Falconer Harrison, eds. *The Wycliffe Bible Commentary.* Chicago: Moody, 1990.

Phipps, Carter. "Progress or Pessimism: How Should We Think about the Future?" May 29, 2013. http://www.carterphipps.com/2013/05/29/progress-or-pessimism-how-should-we-think-about-the-future/.

Pinker, Steven. *The Better Angels of Our Nature: Why Violence Has Decline.* London: Penguin, 2012.

———. *Enlightenment Now: The Case for Reason, Science, Humanism, and Progress.* London: Penguin, 2018.

Piper, John. "Gospel Hope for Cultural Pessimists." *Desiring God,* March 17, 2016. http://www.desiringgod.org/interviews/gospel-hope-for-cultural-pessimists.

———. "Is the Kingdom Present or Future?" *Desiring God,* February 4, 1990. https://www.desiringgod.org/messages/is-the-kingdom-present-or-future.

———. "The Locust Horde and the Day of the Lord." *Desiring God,* September 19, 1982. https://www.desiringgod.org/messages/the-locust-horde-and-the-day-of-the-lord.

Pollock, Doug. *God Space.* Loveland, CO: Group Publishing, 2009.

"Premillennialism Reigns in Evangelical Theology." *National Association of Evangelicals.* January 2011. https://www.nae.net/premillennialism-reigns-in-evangelical-theology/.

Rainer, Thom S. *Autopsy of a Deceased Church: 12 Ways to Keep Yours Alive.* Nashville: B&H, 2014.

Ramachandran, Vilayanur. "The Neurons That Shaped Civilization." TEDIndia video, 7:43. November 2009, Mysore, India. https://www.ted.com/talks/vs_ramachandran_the_neurons_that_shaped_civilization.

Ramirez, Gerardo, and Sian L Beilock. "Writing about Testing Worries Boosts Exam Performance in the Classroom." *Science*, January 14, 2011. http://www.sciencemag.org/content/331/6014/211.abstract.

Reed, Ben. "Why Circles are Better than Rows." *Life & Theology*, November 20, 1012. http://www.benreed.net/why-circles-are-better-than-rows/.

Reeves, Marjorie E. "Joachim of Fiore." https://www.britannica.com/biography/Joachim-of-Fiore.

Riddlebarger, Kim. *A Case for Amillennialism: Understanding the End Times.* Grand Rapids: Baker, 2013.

Roberto, John. "Faith Formation 2020: Designing the Future of Faith." *FaithFormation 2020*, 2010. https://www.lifelongfaith.com/uploads/5/1/6/4/5164069/__ff_2020_handout_-_charlotte.pdf.

Roberts, Richard Owen. *Revival!* Wheaton, IL: Amazon Digital Services, 1991.

Robins, Ali. "8 Reasons Why You Might Be a Bad Boss (And How to Fix it)." *Officevibe*, May 11, 2017. https://www.officevibe.com/blog/facts-about-bad-bosses-infographic.

Rosling, Hans. *Factfulness: Ten Reasons We're Wrong about the World.* New York: Flatiron, 2018.

Ross, Tamie. "MetroChurch Members OK Life Church Merger." *Newsok.com*, January 8, 2001. https://newsok.com/article/2726022/metrochurch-members-ok-life-church-merger.

"S. Parkes Cadman Dies in Coma at 71." *The New York Times*, July 12, 1936. https://www.nytimes.com/1936/07/13/archives/s-parkes-cadman-dies-in-coma-at-71-brooklyn-pastor-first-of-radio.html.

Scheier, Michael F., and Charles Carver. "Effects of Optimism on Psychological and Physical Well-Being: Theoretical Overview and Empirical Update." *Cognitive Therapy and Research* 16 (1992) 201–28. http://doi.org/10.1007/BF01173489.

Schirrmacher, Thomas. "Persecution and Mission." *Lausanne World Pulse Archives*, November 2008. http://www.lausanneworldpulse.com/themedarticles-php/1048/11-2008.

Schmitz, Taylor W., et al. "Opposing Influences of Affective State Valence on Visual Cortical Encoding." *Journal of Neuroscience* 29 (2009) 7199–7207.

Schnabel, Landon, and Sean Bock. "The Persistent and Exceptional Intensity of American Religion: A Response to Recent Research." *Sociological Science*, November 27, 2017. https://www.sociologicalscience.com/download/vol-4/november/SocSci_v4_686to700.pdf.

Schultz, Thom. *Why Nobody Wants to Go to Church Anymore: And How 4 Acts of Love Will Make Your Church Irresistible.* N.p.: Group Publishing, 2013. Kindle.

Schwartz, Barry. *The Paradox of Choice: Why More is Less.* New York: HarperCollins, 2014.

Schwartz, Tony. "Overcoming Your Negative Bias." *New York Times*, June 14, 2013. https://dealbook.nytimes.com/2013/06/14/overcoming-your-negativity-bias/.

Schwartz, Tony, et al. *Be Excellent at Anything: The Four Keys to Transforming the Way We Work and Live.* New York: Free Press, 2011.

Shattuck, Kelly. "7 Startling Facts: An Up-Close Look at Church Attendance in America." *ChurchLeaders*, July 19, 2018. https://churchleaders.com/pastors/pastor-articles/139575-7-startling-facts-an-up-close-look-at-church-attendance-in-america.html.

Shore, Nick. "Turning on the 'No-Collar' Workforce." *MediaDailyNews*, March 12, 2012. http://www.mediapost.com/publications/article/170109/turning-on-the-no-collar-workforce.html.

Singleton, John. "At the Roots of Methodism: Wesley Discovers Field Preaching." *The Christian Post*, March 28, 2003. https://www.christianpost.com/news/at-the-roots-of-methodism-wesley-discovers-field-preaching-6006/.

Skeldon, Grant. *The Passion Generation*. Grand Rapids: Zondervan, 2018.

Smietana, Bob. "Only One-Third of Pastors Share 'Left Behind' End Times Theology." *Christianity Today*, April 26, 2016. https://www.christianitytoday.com/news/2016/april/sorry-left-behind-pastors-end-times-rapture-antichrist.html.

———. "Statistical Illusion." *Christianity Today*, April 1, 2006. http://www.christianitytoday.com/ct/2006/april/32.85.html.

Smitha, Frank E. "Britain in the Mid-1700s." http://www.fsmitha.com/h3/h29-fr.htm.

Sosnik, Doug. "America's Hinge Moment." *POLITICO*, March 29, 2015. http://www.politico.com/magazine/story/2015/03/2016-predictions-americas-sosnik-clinton-116480.

Soto, Alonso. "Chile to Dig Escape Shaft, Prep Miners for Long Haul." *Reuters*, August 24, 2010. https://www.reuters.com/article/us-chile-mine-accident-idUSTRE67N4P820100824.

Sowell, Thomas. "Random Thoughts." *The Patriot Post*, August 11, 2009. https://patriotpost.us/opinion/3215-random-thoughts-2009-08-11.

Sproul, R. C. *The Last Days According to Jesus: When Did Jesus Say He Would Return?* Grand Rapids: Baker, 2015.

———. "Predestination and Evangelism." *Ligoneer Ministries*. https://www.ligonier.org/learn/devotionals/predestination-and-evangelism/.

Spurgeon, Charles H. *The Treasury of David*. Lynchburg, VA: Old-Time Gospel Hour, 1985.

Stanley, Andy. *Deep & Wide: Creating Churches Unchurched People Love to Attend*. Grand Rapids: Zondervan, 2016.

Stanley, Brian. "Winning the World: Carey and the Modern Missionary Movement." *Christianity Today*, December 22, 1986. http://www.christianitytoday.com/history/issues/issue-9/winning-world-carey-and-modern-missionary-movement.html.

Stetzer, Edward. *Christians in the Age of Outrage: How to Bring our Best When the World is at its Worst*. Carol Stream, IL: Tyndale House, 2018.

Stetzer, Edward, and Phillip Connor. "How Many Church Plants Really Survive—And Why?" CP Study.2. https://www.google.com/url?sa=t&rct=j&q=&esrc=s&source=web&cd=&ved=2ahUKEwj0g92KroPsAhUPJzQIHbQMAOEQFjAAegQIAhAB&url=https%3A%2F%2Fwww.christianitytoday.com%2Fassets%2F10228.pdf&usg=AOvVaw1hxLrnTeeHwEx0a01Tlos1.

Stetzer, Edward, and Warren Bird. "The State of Church Planting in the United States: Research Overview and Qualitative Study of Primary Church Planting Entities." http://www.christianitytoday.com/assets/10228.pdf.

Strand, Paul. "Time for a Second Reformation? Why Some Say Another 'Revival' is Not Enough." *The Christian Broadcasting Network*, February 4, 2018. www1.cbn.com/cbnnews/us/2018/february/time-for-a-second-reformation-why-some-say-another-revival-is-not-enough.

Stuckert, Brian L. "Strategic Implications of American Millennialism." Fort Leavenworth, KS: School of Advanced Military Studies, 2008.

Sweeney, Jon M. "Leonard Sweet on Signs, Signals, Churches and the Current State of Starbucks." *ExploreFaith.org*, 2011. http://www.explorefaith.org/faces/my_faith/leonard_sweet.php.

Sweet, Leonard. *AquaChurch 2.0: Piloting Your Church in Today's Fluid Culture*. Colorado Springs: David C. Cook, 2008.

———. "Because I Suspect Some of Our 22nd Century Kids May Live to Be 170, I Looked at What the Church was Talking about 170 Years Ago. . . ." *Facebook*. September 16, 2017. https://www.facebook.com/lensweet/posts/10154753804671791.

———, "Better to Be Wrong about Something Big than Right about Trivialities." *Facebook*, September 2, 2018. https://www.facebook.com/lensweet/posts/10155506223096791.

———. *Giving Blood: A Fresh Paradigm for Preaching*. Grand Rapids: Zondervan, 2014.

———. *The Gospel According to Starbucks: Living with a Grande Passion*. Colorado Springs: WaterBrook, 2008. Kindle.

———. "Leonard Sweet on the Future of the Church." *Facts & Trends*, May 8, 2014. http://factsandtrends.net/2014/05/08/leonard-sweet-on-the-future-of-the-church/#.WFQ9EHeZNE5.

———. *Nudge: Awakening Each Other to the God Who's Already There*. Colorado Springs: David C. Cook, 2010.

———. *Soul Tsunami: Sink or Swim in New Millennium Culture*. Grand Rapids: Zondervan, 1999.

———. *Viral: How Social Networking is Poised to Ignite Revival*. Colorado Springs: WaterBrook, 2012. Kindle.

Sweet, Leonard, and Frank Viola. *Jesus: A Theography*. Nashville: Thomas Nelson, 2012.

Tennent, Timothy C. *Theology in the Context of World Christianity*. Grand Rapids: Zondervan, 2007.

Tennyson, Ken. "Semiotic Awareness." *Transforming Society*, April 29, 2007. http://transformingsociety.blogspot.com/2007/04/semiotic-awareness.html.

Tickle, Phyllis. *The Age of the Spirit: How the Ghost of an Ancient Controversy is Shaping the Church*. Grand Rapids: Baker, 2014.

Tickle, Phyllis, and Danielle Shroyer. *The Great Emergence: How Christianity is Changing and Why*. Grand Rapids: Baker, 2012.

Tracy, Joseph. *The Great Awakening: A History of the Revival of Religion in the Time of Edwards and Whitefield*. N.p.: Counted Faithful, 2014. Kindle Edition.

Tulgan, Bruce. "Meet Generation Z: The Second Generation within the Giant 'Millennial' Cohort." *Rainmaker Thinking*, October 2013. http://www.rainmakerthinking.com/assets/uploads/2013/10/Gen-Z-Whitepaper.pdf.

Tupy, Marian L. "An Update on the Global State of Human Freedo." *Human Progress*, June 15, 2016. https://humanprogress.org/article.php?p=297.

———. "Hollywood's Apocalypse Obsession Ignores Reality." *Human Progress*, June 18, 2019. https://humanprogress.org/article.php?p=1982.

———. "Hong Kong and the Power of Economic Freedom." *Human Progress*, March 7, 2016. https://humanprogress.org/article.php?p=187.

———. "How Humanity Won the War on Famine." *Human Progress*, August 16, 2018. https://humanprogress.org/article.php?p=1459.

———. "Is Moral Progress Real or Just a Myth?" *Human Progress*, January 18, 2019. https://humanprogress.org/article.php?p=1674.

———. "Things are Getting Better, So Why are We All So Gloomy?" *Human Progress,* January 6, 2018. https://humanprogress.org/article.php?p=1084.

Tyra, Gary. *A Missional Orthodoxy: Theology and Ministry in a Post-Christian Context.* Downers Grove, IL: InterVarsity, 2013.

Valentine, McKinley. "Chronos & Kairos." https://mckinleyvalentine.com/kairos/.

Van Buskirk, Greg. "John Wesley's Practical Eschatology." Paper delivered at the Boston University School of Theology Doctoral Conference, Boston, MA, March 24, 2012. https://www.academia.edu/4066589/John_Wesley_s_Practical_Eschatology.

Veith, Gene Edward. "When Truth Gets Left Behind." *Christian Research Journal,* August 15, 2014. https://www.equip.org/article/when-truth-gets-left-behind/.

Venema, Cornelis P. "Revelation 20: Part IV—The Believer's Reign with Christ." https://graceonlinelibrary.org/eschatology/revelation-20/revelation-20-part-iv-the-believers-reign-with-christ-by-cornelis-p-venema/.

Wang, Brian. "Poverty in Numbers: The Changing State of Global Poverty from 2005 to 2015 by the Brookings Institute." *Next Big Future,* February 27, 2011. https://www.nextbigfuture.com/2011/02/poverty-in-numbers-changing-state-of.html.

War Conference. "Final Statement of the War Conference." Cornell Library, February 28, 1988. https://rmc.library.cornell.edu/HRC/exhibition/stage/REX023_164.pdf.

Wax, Trevin. "Pessimistic about the Future? You Need 'Gospel Bearings.'" *The Gospel Coalition,* January 26, 2017. https://www.thegospelcoalition.org/blogs/trevin-wax/christians-need-gospel-bearings-when-pessimism-is-all-the-rage/.

———. *This is Our Time: Everyday Myths in Light of the Gospel.* Nashville: B&H, 2017.

Wesley, John, "The General Spread of the Gospel." *The Wesley Center Online,* April 28, 2014. https://www.whdl.org/general-spread-gospel-sermon-63?language=en.

———. "The Signs of the Times." *The Wesley Center Online,* July 1, 2014. https://www.whdl.org/signs-times-sermon-66.

"What We Do." *Human Progress.* https://humanprogress.org/about#sec2.

White, James Emery. *Meet Generation Z: Understanding and Reaching the New Post-Christian World.* Grand Rapids: Baker, 2017.

Wilson, Douglas. *Future Men.* Moscow, ID: Canon, 2001.

———. *Heaven Misplaced: Christ's Kingdom on Earth.* Moscow, ID: Canon, 2011.

Wimberly, Russell. *The Changing Face of the Church: New Wineskins for a New Generation.* Self-published: Amazon Digital Services, 2013.

Witt, Jessica K., et al. "Get Me Out of This Slump! Visual Illusions Improve Sports Performance." *Psychological Science* 23 (2012) 397–99.

Wolterstorff, Nicholas. "The Story about Religious Freedom You Haven't Heard." *Cardus.ca,* December 1, 2017. https://www.cardus.ca/comment/article/the-story-about-religious-freedom-you-havent-heard/.

Zylstra, Sarah Eekhoff. "Praise the Lord and Pass the Ammunition, Quantified." *Christianity Today,* July 24, 2017. http://www.christianitytoday.com/news/2017/july/praise-lord-pass-ammunition-who-loves-god-guns-pew.html.